SOCOTRA

HILARY BRADT & JANICE BOOTH
UPDATED BY
CHRIS MILLER & MIRANDA LINDSAY-FYNN

www.bradtguides.com

Bradt Guides Ltd, UK
The Globe Pequot Press Inc, USA

Bradt GUIDES
TRAVEL TAKEN SERIOUSLY

Second edition published January 2025
First published 2020
Bradt Travel Guides Ltd
31a High Street, Chesham, Buckinghamshire, HP5 1BW, England
www.bradtguides.com
Print edition published in the USA by The Globe Pequot Press Inc
PO Box 480, Guilford, Connecticut 06437-0480

Text copyright © Bradt Travel Guides Ltd, 2025
Maps copyright © Bradt Travel Guides Ltd, 2025; includes map data © OpenStreetMap contributors
Photographs copyright © Individual photographers, 2025 (see below)
Project Manager: Elspeth Beidas
Cover research: Pepi Bluck, Perfect Picture

ISBN: 9781804692240

British Library Cataloguing in Publication Data
A catalogue record for this book is available from the British Library

Photographs © individual photographers and organisations credited beside images & also from picture libraries credited as follows: Alamy.com (A); Dreamstime.com (D); Shutterstock.com (S); Superstock.com (SS)

Front cover Bottle tree above Detwah lagoon (Nick Ledger/A)
Back cover, clockwise from top left Dragon's blood tree (Znm/D); Detwah lagoon (Chris Miller); Egyptian vulture (Tilman Schimmel); Ghost crab (Chris Miller)
Title page, clockwise from top left Caralluma socotrana (Chris Miller); Shrubs and woodlands across a valley in the Haggeher mountains (Tilman Schimmel); Socotra cisticola (Chris Miller); Sunset at Shu'ab (Chris Miller)

Maps David McCutcheon FBCart.S. FRGS

Typeset by Ian Spick, Bradt Guides
Production managed by Zenith Media; printed in the UK
Digital conversion by www.dataworks.co.in

Paper used for this product comes from sustainably managed forests, and recycled and controlled sources.

AUTHORS

Hilary Bradt founded Bradt Travel Guides accidentally in 1974 while backpacking with her then-husband George through South America. Though semi-retired, she is still involved with the company, mostly in trying to persuade sceptical staff to publish guides to places no-one has heard of. She assumed that after 30 or so years of roughing it, and an MBE, she had finally earned the right for some comfort, and even managed a stint as lecturer on a luxury ship. But then along came Socotra...

...and Janice Booth, who rather thought she had finished with airport departure lounges and writing books for Bradt, but couldn't resist it. She began proofreading and copy-editing for the company back in 1996, which led to co-writing the first three editions of their Rwanda guide (she had connections there) and, later, three 'Slow' guides to Devon with Hilary.

She died in 2023.

UPDATERS

Chris Miller was born and bred in New Zealand, but after finishing university he followed a job to Australia before moving on to Canada and then London, where he works as a software developer. With so many countries and cultures within easy reach, he has found London to be the perfect base from which to explore the world and his love of travel has grown from there. His interest in photography has evolved naturally alongside the travelling, as he found it the ideal way to capture and share memories and moments from the places he's been.

Miranda Lindsay-Fynn's working life has included being a yacht captain, actively planning voyages and cruises all over the world, including several ocean crossings. Her experience as a captain has helped her develop many useful skills, from celestial navigation to knowing her way around a diesel engine. More recently, she has found her niche as a marketing director for SMEs and start-ups, a world that can be equally as wild and turbulent to navigate as the ocean. In her spare time, she continues to indulge her passion for sailing and frequently travels to extraordinary places with Chris.

I (Hilary) first became aware of Socotra in the 1980s at a talk at the Globetrotters' Club in London, given by the explorer and author Richard Snailham, who had visited the archipelago in – I believe – the '60s. He had to apologise for the quality of the Ectachrome slides, which had faded to a uniform yellow, but even so I can still remember the extraordinary dragon's blood trees and the sand dunes. Decades later the island's vegetation was filmed for a David Attenborough television programme, and I was hooked. I started answering journalists' questions of 'Where do you still want to travel to?' with 'Socotra', and then I'd smile smugly while they wondered whether to admit that they didn't know where it was. When I reached my late 70s I thought I had better start planning before I got too old to manage such a rugged trip.

We (Chris and Miranda) had been dreaming of a trip to Socotra for years, but with no flights available and the only access being via an infrequent and impractical concrete ship, any hopes of reaching the island remained on our backburner until it started to open up again in 2019. Realising that a visit finally seemed achievable, we planned a two-week adventure to help squeeze in as much as possible. A chance sighting of a Twitter post from Bradt Guides shortly before our departure, followed by a very speculative email exchange, revealed that Hilary and Janice would soon be heading there too in preparation for the first edition of this guide. This led to a serendipitous connection, resulting in us somehow contributing to the first edition with photos, maps and trekking stories.

Fast forward three years and Hilary got back in touch with us out of the blue, asking if we would consider returning to Socotra to update a second edition. We didn't hesitate to take up the offer! Socotra's a dream destination and we knew there was still so much more there we wanted to see and do. On our return we weren't disappointed. We managed to catch up with friends old and new, explore a whole range of stunning new routes, regions and activities that weren't covered in the first edition, and generally marvel all over again at just what a magical corner of the world this is. We hope at least some of Socotra's wonder is made apparent through this guide.

Note that the first edition was largely written in the first person from Hilary and Janice's travel experiences, and it was intentionally not always clear whether it's Hilary or Janice writing in the first person. Their first-person writing has been preserved in this 2024 update, but updated text can be distinguished either by the date and 'we' or 'Chris and Miranda found...'.

Contributors

Their contributions are a vital part of this book and we are massively grateful to them all, from our fellow travellers in Socotra to the specialists in various disciplines who have squeezed us generously into their busy schedules, along with others who shared their travel experiences with us and chipped in so readily when we were stuck for some specific fact, detail or location. They were all united – with us – in wanting to do their best for Socotra, and without them you would be reading a much thinner and less interesting book. THANK YOU, everyone.

DONORS The first edition was financed through a crowd-funding campaign because Covid wiped out our publishing budget. A total of 283 donors contributed, and without them this book would not have happened.

FELLOW TRAVELLERS AND INDEPENDENT TRAVELLERS Hilary thanks **fellow travellers** during her and Janice's whistle-stop visit to Socotra, who shared our amazement at the island, took all the surprises cheerfully in their stride and have written their impressions for this book: Sally Crook, Emily Glover, Julian Glover, Liz and Richard Lea, Oona Muirhead and Matthew Parris. We're looking forward to the reunion – and please, travel with us again one day!

Independent travellers who shared their experiences and photos with us: **Chris Miller** and **Nicole Smoot** (more on them on pages iii and vi, as you'll hear their voices, read their experiences and see their photos throughout the book); **Daniel Austin**, whose massive accumulation of knowledge about everything you didn't even know you needed to know (and more) includes Socotra's very beautiful spiders; **Daniel McLaughlin**, who wrote the 2007 Bradt Guide to Yemen which today's tourists still use (we saw them!); **Radwan Mobarak Ali Mohamed** of Socotra Eco-Tours, an experienced Socotri tour operator whose team looked after us on the island and who was Hilary's first point of contact when planning the trip; **Matt Reichel** of Inertia Network, who organised our visit and answered all our many questions so patiently; and **Tony Wheeler**, who gave us helpful information despite being sent home early when flights were cancelled because of Coronavirus.

Chris and Miranda would like to thank **Ruslan Amin Gumaan Ragab**, our guide and friend, who arranged our trip and helped us discover new places and experiences. In no small feat, he also managed to find all of Socotra Island's endemic birds for us, and helped provide and verify plenty of information updates for this second edition. Ruslan is an excellent source of knowledge and can be reached at e ruslan771916@gmail.com or via WhatsApp at m +967 7 7191 6954. We'd also like to thank **Fouad Naseeb Saeed**, who took us diving and shared his expertise on the marine nature sanctuaries; **Ismael Salem**, who invited us for tea and introduced us to the amazing work of the Soqotra Heritage Project, particularly the major initiative to preserve the island's rock art; and **Eisa 'the**

Camel Man', who arranged our camel trek and treated us to a traditional Socotri-style goat dinner.

Matt Reichel, tour operator and photographer Matt is a co-founding member of Inertia Network. He is a geopolitics junkie, photographer and expedition leader from Vancouver, Canada, with degrees in International Relations and East Asian Studies. He is passionate about engaging with post-conflict zones and geopolitical hotspots, having led Inertia programmes in Yemen, Afghanistan, Pakistan, Myanmar and Saudi Arabia among others. He has been involved in setting up eco-tourism and social projects in Socotra since the island re-opened to tourism in early 2018, and authored a report on ecotourism in post-conflict Socotra which can be found on the Inertia website w inertianetwork.com.

Nicole Smoot, photographer, traveller and blogger Nicole was born and raised in Alaska. It was there that she gained an appreciation for extreme areas that has continued to lure her to remote pockets of Alaska, and beyond to places such as Yemen and Tajikistan. In 2015 she began an adventure travel blog, the *Adventures of Lil Nicki* (w adventuresoflilnicki.com), focusing on lesser visited areas after her first trip to Yemen and Socotra the previous year, before going on to work in tourism promotion and development projects in Kazakhstan, Kyrgyzstan, Antarctica and the Dominican Republic. Nicole has also had the opportunity to lead expeditions in Socotra, mainland Yemen, Tajikistan, Afghanistan, Egypt, Pakistan and Xinjiang.

ADVISERS Finally the **expert contributors**, highly qualified in their fields and each one of them knowing far more about Socotra than we could ever hope to learn. You will see their contributions throughout the guide. We've been overwhelmed by their generosity, in terms of time, expertise and general support. Any errors or shortcomings that there may be in the book are most certainly not theirs: we, the authors, take full responsibility.

Benjamin Carey FTS, Carey Tourism An award-winning tourism consultant and former tour operator specialising in destinations emerging from crisis and conflict, Benjamin has experience in more than 50 countries. He focuses on local communities, exploring how renewal of their heritage can provide a foundation for environmental and social justice. He is tourism expert of the Soqotra Heritage Project (page 46), having previously advised Yemen's Ministry of Tourism on strategy and represented the Yemen Tourism Promotion Board in Europe. For the past 15 years Benjamin's work has included championing sustainable tourism on Socotra, to introduce the islands' cultural and natural heritage to the wider world.

Dr Alan Forrest A biodiversity scientist at the Centre for Middle Eastern Plants (CMEP: w cmep.org.uk), part of the Royal Botanic Garden Edinburgh, Alan Forrest started his career with a range of conservation studies using molecular techniques in the UK and Spain. He moved to CMEP in 2012 having reached the realisation that resources used to acquire very detailed knowledge about very few plants could be used to benefit plant conservation more broadly by linking it to community livelihoods, sustainable use, and heritage in its broadest sense – especially in countries with fewer resources and those affected by conflict. He is project manager of the Soqotra Heritage Project, and currently works more widely on conservation projects in Socotra, the Arabian Peninsula and central Asia.

Dr Julian Jansen van Rensburg An archaeologist, photographer and *National Geographic* explorer, Julian has worked on Socotra for over 22 years. He has led numerous multidisciplinary research projects and expeditions to explore and document cultural heritage in some of the most remote places on earth, both underground and underwater. He has recorded and published his discoveries extensively and is an advocate for the protection and management of cultural heritage in terms of local communities, and the importance of dialogue in capacity building, training, advocacy and education. When not away on an expedition he can be found diving in the ocean or enjoying a coffee and a large piece of chocolate cake.

Dr Miranda J Morris An independent researcher based in St Andrew's, Scotland, Dr Morris's interests focus on the ethnography and languages of southern Arabia. She has worked on a variety of projects in the region, most recently a Leverhulme-funded analysis of modern south Arabian languages (page 158), and has researched Socotra extensively. Her latest book on Socotra is *Island Voices: The Oral Art of Soqotra* (page 159), and scattered through this guide you will find her delightful translations of Socotri poetry. Other publications include the encyclopaedic *Ethnoflora of the Soqotra Archipelago* (page 159). Dr Morris helped set up Friends of Soqotra (page 44) and remains an active member.

Richard Porter (e RFPorter@talktalk.net) Richard has visited Socotra many times to study its birdlife and his papers on their populations and distributions can be found in *Sandgrouse*, the journal of the Ornithological Society of the Middle East. He is adviser to BirdLife International's Middle East programme and author of the field guide, *Birds of the Middle East* (which includes all the Socotra birds; page 158) and four other field guides to Middle Eastern countries. He also wrote *Birds and Plants of Socotra* (with Tony Miller) and is a member of Friends of Soqotra. Richard is happy to advise anyone visiting Socotra who wants to watch birds.

Dr Kay Van Damme (e kay.vandamme@gmail.com) A Belgian freshwater biologist who is passionate about Socotra, Kay Van Damme has been actively involved in scientific research, conservation, education and nature awareness in the Socotra archipelago since 1999. He is Chairperson of Friends of Soqotra, was Science Editor of *Socotra: A Natural History of the Islands and Their People* (page 158), and has written and published many scientific papers about the islands (page 160). He has trained several local conservationists and has discovered and described several new species on the island. Returning there almost every two years, he spends most of his time admiring the amazing biodiversity of the island's freshwater animals.

Dr Raquel Vasconcelos (w cibio.up.pt/en/people/details/raquel-vasconcelos) Graduating in Biology in 2003 and attaining her PhD in Biology at the University of Porto (UP), Portugal, in 2011, Dr Raquel Vasconcelos is currently a researcher at the UP's CIBIO/InBIO (Research Centre in Biodiversity and Genetic Resources). Her research focuses on supporting island conservation, using reptiles as models, by combining ecological modelling techniques with morphological and genetic data. Her doctoral thesis was on the systematics of reptiles in the Cabo Verde Islands and her postdoctoral fellowship focused on conserving genetic diversity in hotspot islands of biodiversity, this time using the reptiles of the Socotra archipelago as models. She has also been responsible for/involved in various activities to increase scientific knowledge and demystify the non-specialised public's image of reptiles.

Contents

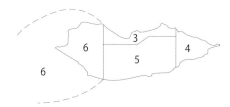

Sand dunes at Zaheq (page 134) (Chris Miller)

MAP LIST

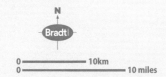

N

Bradt

| 0 | 10km |
| 0 | 10 miles |

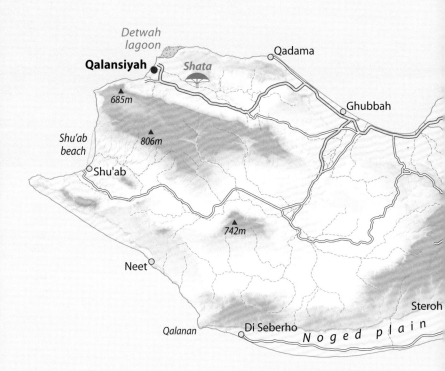

Detwah lagoon

Qalansiyah ●

Shata

○ Qadama

▲ 685m

○ Ghubbah

Shu'ab beach

▲ 806m

○ Shu'ab

▲ 742m

Neet ○

▲

Steroh

Qalanan

Di Seberho ○ *Noged plain*

A R A B I A N

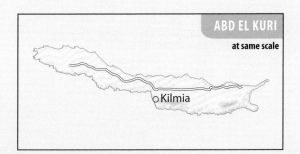

ABD EL KURI

at same scale

○ Kilmia

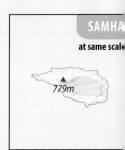

SAMHA

at same scale

▲ 779m

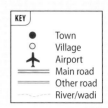

● Town
○ Village
✈ Airport
═══ Main road
─── Other road
--- River/wadi

Hawlaf (port)

Delisha

Suq

diboh

Qaria lagoon

aft Canyon
tional Park

1105m ▲

▲ 1354m

Skand
1495m ▲

Haggeher mountains

Komhil Nature
Sanctuary

Riqeleh

Hoq Cave

Jo'oh

sam
teau

▲ 863m

Firmihin
Forest

Arher

Nissam

Ras Erissel

Momi Plateau

Dakam
Forest

sam

Matyaf

Dagub
Cave

Aomak

Zaheq

DARSA

at same scale

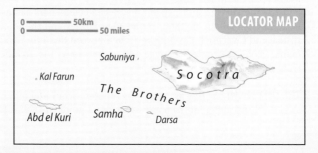

0 ═══ 50km
0 ═══ 50 miles

LOCATOR MAP

Sabuniya

Kal Farun

Socotra

The Brothers

Abd el Kuri

Samha

Darsa

Introduction

It was a close thing. We, the original authors, spent a breathless week in 2020 being driven around Socotra with a group of friends, cramming in as much as our itinerary would allow. We walked, climbed, swam, camped, picnicked, boated, talked, photographed, asked endless questions – and not a moment too soon. Less than a month after our return, Coronavirus struck, flights to the island stopped and no more tourist visas were issued. Chris and Miranda, who described their camel trek in 2020, returned in 2024 to explore new places and note changes in familiar ones.

So, this is a book of many voices. The voices of our fellow travellers (and other recent Socotra visitors) are here, and those of the Socotri people, and most particularly those of the specialists in so many fields who have pitched in generously with their time and expertise. We hope that Socotra's own voices are here too, in the glimpses we have given of its fascinating history, the art scratched by ancient people on the walls of hidden caves, the poetry passed down lovingly from age to age, landscapes frozen in time where herders have led their flocks through countless generations, and coasts where seafarers and traders from so long ago sailed their ships in search of the precious myrrh, frankincense, aloe and crimson dragon's blood this tiny island could provide. A book of many voices, with so many things to say.

THE ISLAND Although barely larger than the English county of Cornwall, Socotra is by far the biggest of the four islands in the Socotra archipelago and the one geared for tourism at the time of writing. Shaped like a rather wobbly trilby hat, with a high crown in the middle encircled by a flattish brim, it's a storehouse of wonderful oddities: craggy peaks where buzzards soar, giant sand dunes, seriously obese desert roses (*Adenium obesum*), dragon's blood trees like old-fashioned darning mushrooms and colourful crabs in hidden inland streams. And such beauty, everywhere you look.

Back in the days of sail, when trading ships from many nations (including those of the East India Company) billowed their way around the Indian Ocean and Arabian Sea, Socotra was well placed on their routes. Then the opening of the Suez Canal in 1869 brought more P&O passenger and cargo ships from Britain into the waters. One, built on Tyneside and launched in 1896, was even named *The Socotra*. Most of these passenger ships steamed on by with just a passing glance at the islands, but in 1897 the SS *Aden* (page 112) was one of the less fortunate…

Then the surveys and expeditions began: Lieutenant James Wellsted in 1834, Isaac Bayley Balfour in 1880, Henry Ogg Forbes and the joint expedition of the British and Liverpool museums in 1898. Between them they amassed data on flora, fauna, geology, people, language and archaeology; the archipelago was well and truly studied.

THE DIFFERENCES Just as Socotra is different from any other Bradt destination, so is this book different from any other Bradt guide. Its aim is to entertain, inform and inspire – particularly to inspire – but not necessarily to help with your travel in our usual way. You won't need that. Remember that Socotra is a UNESCO World Heritage Site and carefully protected. To get a flight to the island you (currently) need a tourist visa, which can only be issued by one of the island's own tour operators. If you are arranging your holiday through an international tour operator, they will be working with one of these. You can opt either to join a scheduled tour or to have an itinerary tailor-made for you, whether alone or with friends; but, either way, when you are on the island you will be looked after by a local guide and following one or other pre-arranged itinerary. For this and other good reasons of conservation and protection (the island's, not yours!), Socotra is not ideal for the go-it-alone traveller.

Therefore we give minimal information about transport, accommodation, where to eat and so forth, because your tour operator will have all that in hand. We just make you aware of the choices and attractions available, against a general background of the island and its flora, fauna, history, landscapes and people. Many potential sites are not yet on the tourist circuit; they will open up as tourism increases but this can – and should – only happen slowly, as and when the local people feel ready. If some don't want their villages visited, that's their legitimate choice.

Meanwhile there is so much to discover, so much richness in such a small area. Enjoy the descriptions and the wonderful photos taken by Chris, Matt, Nicole and others (page iii and page vi), and dream of going there someday, just as I (Hilary) did a decade or more ago. I made it finally, and so can you. And even if you never get there, your life will still be richer for knowing about it.

THE TOURIST EXPERIENCE Socotra is known for its natural environment. That's why it's a UNESCO World Heritage Site and why savvy travellers want to go there, and given the cost of even a short trip it is likely that those who are serious about doing so will have been to many of the world's other natural-history destinations: Africa, Madagascar, the Galápagos Islands, Costa Rica... They will have experienced some of the best local wildlife guides in the world and will have come to expect a high level of local knowledge to inform and influence their trip. This is not how it works in Socotra. The island simply hasn't had the time, money or commitment to train enough local people as expert guides in the subjects that most interest tourists: the flora and fauna. That's the main reason we, Hilary and Janice, wrote this book – it's the one we wish we'd had before we travelled to this beguiling island. We were woefully underprepared.

You may be lucky and be allocated one of the island's experts in the subject that interests you. Some excellent guides do exist, but not enough to provide for every group. Also, the best tend to get head-hunted to more lucrative jobs elsewhere. But if political stability returns and tourism continues to increase, this situation should start to improve.

Then there's the 'accommodation'. At the time of writing there are seven hotels, all in or near Hadiboh, five of them fairly basic and the other two a cut above (page 77). More are on the drawing board, in response to the increasing numbers of tourists that are visiting the island. Outside Hadiboh or the eco-lodge at Delisha (page 87) you'll generally sleep in tents, provided by your tour operator. While most of the more popular campsites have at least basic bathroom and cooking facilities these days, not all do, and many places are strictly 'back to nature', with no facilities at all.

So those are the negatives. The positives are the wonderful Socotri crew who do their absolute best to make the trip unforgettable and to keep their foreign visitors

You have probably already spotted So**c**otra spelt with a 'c' and So**q**otra with a 'q', and that's just the tip of the iceberg. Almost every place name on the island can be seen with various spellings. Within this book we have tried to be consistent, but you will come across variations elsewhere. *Soqotra*, for example, which we use only when it's in the name of an organisation or website, is preferred linguistically and by the Socotri/Soqotri people themselves, and you will see it in academic publications; so we faced a dilemma, because *Socotra* with a 'c' is (rightly or wrongly) more commonly used around the world and in relation to tourism, whereas the 'q' (particularly without a 'u') would be less familiar for some readers. We – and Bradt Guides – opted for familiarity. As Dr Miranda Morris explains (page 37), Socotri was a spoken language, not a written one, so names were recorded phonetically. Qalansiyah, for example, has been rendered as Colosseah (by James Wellsted in 1834), Gollonsir (Balfour, 1880), Kalenzia and many more. Where versions are very different, as with Suq (east of Hadiboh) which is Shiq in Socotri, we generally give both; otherwise places should be recognisable despite the variation (Hadiboh/Hadibu, Haggeher/Haghier, etc). It sometimes helps to say them aloud.

well fed, safe and comfortable. Ours loved helping the old ladies! We were both looked after and supported (and sometimes hauled along!) on tricky trails with devotion and good humour (see photo, page 57). And our meals, though perhaps a touch monotonous, were thoughtfully prepared and made best use of the relatively limited local ingredients. The biggest positive of all, of course, is the island itself, as we very much hope you will discover.

THE DIFFICULTIES A further 'unknown' for Socotra comes from the endlessly fluctuating political situation (page 36). As we hand the book over to the printers, in November 2024, the archipelago is still a part of Yemen; but we don't know which regime will be in control by the time you read this, nor what their attitude to tourism will be. We don't know where you will fly from to Socotra, with which airline, or who will provide your visa. We've no reason to think that the changes, if any, will be damaging, and once on the island visitors may in fact notice very little difference: it will still be the same superbly beautiful place, it will be safe, and you'll still be looked after by a delightful, friendly, hard-working Socotri team who want you to enjoy your stay. However – and it's very frustrating for us as guidebook writers – we can't give you the details. All we can do is wish you a thoroughly good visit. Enjoy!

Looking down to Wadi Da'asqalah from the climb up to Roukab Plateau (page 117) (Chris Miller)

Part One

GENERAL INFORMATION

Nation Yemen Republic

Flag (Yemen) Horizontal bands of red, white, black

Status (Socotra Governorate) One of Yemen's 21 governorates

Political divisions (Socotra Governorate) Two Districts, Hadiboh & Qalansiyah

Other islands in archipelago Abd el Kuri, Darsa, Samha (all in Qalansiyah district)

Location (Socotra island) Arabian Sea/Indian Ocean; approx 250km from Somalia and 380km from mainland Yemen

Size/Area (Socotra island) 3,796km^2/1,466 square miles

Climate Tropical, desert climate, but influenced greatly by altitude; mean annual temperature on lowlands above 25°C/77°F. Strong monsoon winds June to September

Population 100–110,000

Capital Hadiboh (pop approx 15,000)

Other main towns Qalansiyah

Languages Arabic and Socotri

Religion Islam

Currency Yemeni rial

Exchange rate Strong fluctuations: US$1 = 1,800YR (August 2024). Note the rate you see online, currently US$1 = 250YR, is an official rate that is much worse than what you'll get in Hadiboh.

National airline/airport Yemenia Airways/Socotra airport

Telephone code (Socotra) + 967 (0)5

Time GMT+3

Electrical voltage 220V

Electrical sockets UK 3-pin and/or continental 2-pin

Main occupations Fishery, animal husbandry, trade, tourism

Tourist attractions UNESCO World Heritage site; flora and fauna with high percentage of endemism

1

Background Information

I counsel you all, if you will be guided by me: Take good care of your mountain homelands. Keep them pure and unsullied, and see that their good fortune and virtue never leaves them.

Advice of the Socotri ancestors (translation by Miranda Morris)

THE SOCOTRA ARCHIPELAGO

The Socotra (or Soqotra) archipelago lies around 250km off the horn of Africa and 380km from Yemen, its administrative parent. It consists of four islands: Abd el Kuri, Samha and Darsa (for more details of these three, see page 152) and Socotra, by far the largest, around 135km long and 42km wide – roughly the same size and shape as Cornwall. Although the smaller islands have some notable endemic species, it's Socotra which is of particular interest to naturalists for its high level of endemism and strikingly unusual landscapes. In 2008 the archipelago was designated a UNESCO World Heritage Site for its unique biodiversity. Its strategically useful position, poised between the Indian Ocean and the Arabian Sea and within reach of shipping routes between India, East Africa, Suez and the Middle Eastern states, has made it of interest to many countries over the centuries, with the United Arab Emirates and Saudi Arabia currently paying it close attention.

GEOLOGY, LANDSCAPE AND CLIMATE

'A pile of mountains almost surrounded by a low plain' is how 26-year-old Lieutenant James Wellsted of the East India Company's Marine Service described Socotra in 1834, but the island's geological makeup is somewhat more complicated, spanning many ages and many rock formations.

The **Haggeher mountains** with their rearing granite peaks and deep ravines give the island much of its distinctive character and beauty: their highest point, Jebel Skand, reaches 1,550m above sea level. Often swathed in the clouds which nurture its lush forests, this mountain range influences the climate throughout the island. From the highlands, most of the rivers run northward and flow year round because of heavy seasonal rainfall; the consequent availability of fresh water is one reason why the island's north coast has a larger number of settlements than elsewhere. The **limestone plateaux** are notable for areas of karst and conceal an extensive cave system – likened by a Swiss speleologist to Gruyère cheese – much of it still unexplored. Caves here and in the coastal cliffs have provided shelter for livestock and people down the ages, and some are still used.

Coastal plains along the eastern and western sides are windswept and arid, with massive dunes of sugar-white sand blown in from the shore. The inhospitable southern plain, broader than that of the north and much of it scrubby desert, has little fresh water and a low population but ends in some superb sandy beaches, backed by impressive cliffs and yet more dunes.

Looking at Socotra on a map, it's hard to believe that one small island has space for so many different **landscapes**, and indeed they do sometimes merge unexpectedly into one another: desert scrub may butt abruptly against weathered cliffs or be lapped by creamy Indian Ocean breakers, and windswept mountain plateaux crack suddenly into dizzily steep ravines. On the ground, however, the space seems infinite, and distances far greater than in fact they are. Dragon's blood trees, like fuzzy-headed darning mushrooms, co-habit on lonely hillsides with smooth, plump, endearingly human and quite un-rose-like desert roses, while Egyptian vultures hover overhead and goats pursue their single-minded search for food. And these assorted landscapes, whichever way you look, are astonishingly, breathtakingly and quite unmatchably beautiful, with the colours – pink/orange limestone, silver sand dunes, washed-out sky, red sandstone, grey-green scrubby grass, fringes of blue ocean – blending gently together.

Very much less gentle, however, is the **climate**, which effectively limits this perfection – and the tourist season – to just a few months a year, with the wind a powerful enemy. At any time it may be uncomfortably strong, but from June to September fierce monsoon winds bring the seasonal rain and floods, most dramatically in the highlands in the form of violent thunderstorms. Storms batter the coastal areas, and many inhabitants from the outlying islands spend this season on Socotra rather than risk being cut off. Cyclones seem to be increasing in frequency and strength: one (named Megh) in November 2015 proved unusually catastrophic, destroying 500 homes and damaging 3,000 more, smashing dragon's blood trees and demolishing much of the emerging tourism infrastructure; while in May 2018 cyclone Mekunu damaged the port and sank supply ships carrying food. The number of rusting wrecks scattered along the coast are a visible reminder of the weather's power over this small and isolated island group.

NATURAL HISTORY

THE BEGINNING Hundreds of millions of years ago, Africa, Arabia and India sat snugly together, along with South America, Antarctica and Australia, to form the largest continent the earth has ever seen: Gondwana. This was the age of the reptiles, and of ferns, cycads and conifers. Then, perhaps around 200 million years ago, the sea level rose, tectonic plates shifted and Gondwana started to break apart, forming the southern continents we know today. Socotra was part of that plate and was stranded in the ocean as the Gulf of Aden opened up into the Red Sea at least 18 million years ago, settling in its current position at the triple junction of the Gondwanan plates of India, Arabia and Africa. Unlike that other island of endemism, Madagascar, Socotra was too small to provide a home for the evolving mammals (or, if ever present, they have gone extinct and left no trace) but, within this small area, the extraordinary height of its Haggeher mountains – over 1,500m at their peak – together with the climatic variations, created a range of habitats that enabled a variety of plants and small fauna to flourish and evolve into separate species.

FLORA *This section has been provided by Alan Forrest (page vi)*
Despite the relative isolation of Socotra – which being a continental fragment rather than of volcanic origin was never a 'blank slate' for evolution compared with other well-known island groups with high endemism – the plants have been relatively well studied and recorded since the first expeditions in the 19th century.

Vegetation zones Several broad categories are commonly used to classify the vegetation of Socotra, and these are often found in altitudinal zones that intergrade with each other forming mosaics in different areas. Some of the wadis and passes, such as the walk up to Hoq Cave or, more dramatically, the trek to Skand, leading from the coastal plain to the Haggeher, contain examples of all the altitudinal shrubland and woodland types.

Although not a distinct vegetation 'type', the **cliffs** of Socotra harbour some unique and unusual plants that are often sheltered from grazing and browsing animals while still catching the mist and fog so essential to their survival.

The broad categories of vegetation are briefly described here:

Coastal vegetation Perhaps the most threatened vegetation on Socotra, mostly as a result of development. It forms a very narrow strip around the island. Small areas of mangroves remain in the southwest and northwest although much reduced, and the coastal plants can be diverse and differ from area to area.

Croton shrubland Occurring at low altitude up to 100m and dominated by species of the genus Croton, all of which are endemic. The shrubs rarely exceed 2m in height, with occasional trees and a sparse herb layer. It is quite widespread on the coastal plains and the Zahr basin. In some areas the shrubs lean at an oblique angle, possibly reflecting the direction of the prevailing monsoon winds.

Succulent shrubland This is the most recognisable – and special to Socotra – of the vegetation and famed for the 'bottle trees'. It is typical of a sparsely vegetated arid environment, and is mostly found in the foothills and lower slopes of the mountains and escarpments. While generally found at these low elevations, there are higher examples especially on the outer islands. The shrubs can be up to 4m, with emergent trees and cushion plants below, dominated by the common *Jatropha unicostata* (page 108), and various succulents as well as tree succulents such as the desert rose, cucumber tree and euphorbia.

Semi-evergreen woodland Dense thickets to 5m with emergent trees, found along the margins of the plateaux and in the wadis, cliffs and slopes up to 750m. Not common and never found in very large stands.

Woody-based open herb vegetation A mosaic of woody herbs, dwarf shrubs and open grasses less than 2m tall with occasional relict woodlands. A widespread vegetation predominantly on the limestone plateaux.

Submontane shrubland vegetation Semi-deciduous shrubs with emergent *Dracaena cinnabari* (dragon's blood trees) found almost exclusively on the plateaux below the Haggeher to the south and west with occasional outlying areas.

Montane mosaic vegetation Found almost exclusively in the Haggeher mountains – many species are found nowhere else – with different areas containing evergreen woodland, grasses, dwarf shrubland and cushion plants at higher elevations. The best conserved areas can be extremely dense. The evergreen woodland dominated by *Dracaena* is a unique area, found on the higher slopes of the mountains.

Unusual and endemic species Currently 848 vascular plant species are recognised and, of these, 316 (37%) are endemic (ie: found nowhere else on earth), giving it a level of plant endemism comparable with some of the most isolated and diverse islands anywhere. This, of course, may change; there is no doubt that new plant species await discovery on Socotra, and also some of those currently considered endemic will be discovered growing in adjacent regions of Africa and Arabia as has already been the case with several species.

The diverse topography and climate of Socotra matches the diversity of the plants and the areas in which they grow. Some of the plants are unusual even compared with their closest relatives – the cucumber tree (see below and page 8) being a spectacular example. Other groups harbour a number of endemic species that have radiated on the island, some of them relatively recently and some over long periods of geological time. Wet areas that depend upon the fog and mist of the monsoons harbour high numbers of endemic species, some of which are very spatially restricted in their distribution. There are dry endemic areas as well.

Most famous of all Socotra flora is, of course *Dracaena cinnabari* – the **Socotran dragon's blood tree**. Related to other dragon trees found in the Canary Islands, Madeira, Cape Verde, Morocco, Arabia and Africa, and southeast Asia, the Socotri species is the only one known to form extensive woodland. It is threatened through climate change and land management practices leading to overgrazing. All visitors will be taken to Firmihin Forest to see the trees since they are all mature and large, thus photogenic, but in fact they are threatened through over-maturity and a lack of regeneration. You have to go to the steep slopes of the high Haggeher Mountains to see woodland with a good age structure and young plants. It is widely believed that an excess of goats eat the young seedlings, preventing regeneration, and while this is true to an extent, the trees are also suffering from a drying of the climate and a reduction in the monsoon mists and fogs on which they depend for moisture – hence their abundance at higher altitudes where they will no doubt survive another climatic onslaught.

Apart from the iconic dragon's blood trees, the most recognisable components of the landscape are what can be termed bottle trees, a name applied to several unrelated species – the **cucumber tree** (*Dendrosicyos socotranus*) being one. It can attain large dimensions, has a massive swollen trunk and is relatively widespread, despite the fact that it is extensively lopped for fodder and has been almost cleared in some areas. Interestingly, it belongs in the family Cucurbitaceae, the gourd family, and is the only tree species in a family which is predominantly made up of climbers and vines. Molecular research has determined that this tree is an ancient lineage – existing prior to the opening up of the Gulf of Aden and the separation of Socotra as an island. If it previously grew on what

THE ROYAL BOTANIC GARDEN EDINBURGH AND SOCOTRA

Alan Forrest

Although the Socotra Archipelago has been well known throughout history for its strategic position and its involvement in ancient trade routes, the scientific exploration of the island only started in the mid 19th century. The first major expedition was conducted in 1880, led by Isaac Bayley Balfour – later to become Regius Keeper and Queen's Botanist at the Royal Botanic Garden Edinburgh (RBGE) where he remained until 1922 – and assisted by Alexander Scott who was a horticulturalist at RBGE at the time. They spent 48 days on the island. Balfour's *Botany of Socotra* – published in 1888 – described over 200 species and 20 genera new to science, many of them endemic to the islands. He made a number of important collections for horticulture, notably *Begonia socotrana* that is the only winter-flowering begonia known globally. It was cultivated in Edinburgh and crossed to produce hybrid cultivars with South African begonias to establish all known winter-flowering varieties now in cultivation.

A number of additional expeditions were conducted in the later 19th and early 20th century, and then sporadically while British interests remained in Aden. In the 1980s, Yemen – and Socotra – started to open up to the wider world following civil war. RBGE's Tony Miller first visited Socotra in 1989 and undertook an extensive series of botanical and ethnographic surveys alongside Miranda Morris, leading to the publication of the *Ethnoflora of the Soqotra Archipelago* (page 159) in 2006. This work not only documents the plants of Socotra, but also all their traditional uses. RBGE led and contributed to several international expeditions working alongside Socotri partners, making a significant contribution to both the World Heritage Site designation in 2008 and the Socotra Conservation Zoning Plan embedded in Yemeni legislation in 2000. As a result, the herbarium at RBGE contains the best collection of preserved plant specimens from Socotra in the world.

More recently, RBGE projects have undertaken repeat and additional surveys, research on the molecular evolution of the endemic flora, and implementation of the Soqotra Heritage Project (page 46), which has recognised the relationship between the cultural and natural heritages of Socotra and brought heritage awareness and knowledge to a new level. It should also be acknowledged that several other individuals and institutes have undertaken valuable botanical research and conservation activities on Socotra, often working alongside each other with Socotri partners.

is now mainland Arabia, it is no longer there and has likely been isolated on Socotra for the entire lifetime of the island. Other bottle trees include *Adenium obesum* subsp. *sokotranum,* also known as the **desert rose** owing to its large and attractive pink flowers, and *Dorstenia gigas* or **Socotran fig**, which has the appearance of some magical plant from an ancient herbal remedy with its clusters of wrinkled leaves and swollen stems.

There are many endemic **succulent** species as well, and several **orchids**. The most remarkable succulent is perhaps *Duvaliandra dioscorides*, an asclepiad, which grows in a very specialised and rare niche – dry and exposed south-facing slabs of granite in an otherwise wet habitat. This is an unusual place to find a succulent plant, and it is critically endangered due to having extremely low numbers in a very small area – the details of which are deliberately kept secret by local communities.

1 Socotran dragon's blood tree, *Dracaena cinnabari*. The genus is found in other countries but the Socotran species is the only one to form forests (Chris Miller)

2 Cucumber tree, one of the island's several 'bottle trees' (Vladimir Melnik/D)

3 Socotran fig, another bottle tree (Lisa Banfield)

4 The spectacular *Duvaliandra dioscorides* (Lisa Banfield)

5 Aloes have been cultivated on Socotra for centuries (Sergey Strelkov/D)

6 *Geranium biuncinnatum* found after rain in semi-evergreen woodland (Lisa Banfield)

7 *Boswellia elongata*, one of eleven species of frankincense tree found in Socotra (Lisa Banfield)

8 The intensely irritating hairs on *Hibiscus dioscoridis* have led this rare shrub's name to be synonymous with an irritating person in the Socotri language! (Lisa Banfield)

9 *Trichodesma laxiflorum* is one of three species of this genera on the island; the flowers can be white or blue (Chris Miller)

10 *Hypericum scopulorum* is related to the St John's wort. It grows on the higher slopes of the Haggeher mountains (Lisa Banfield)

11 *Oldenlandia pulvinata* (family Rubiaceae) commonly found in croton shrubland (Hilary Bradt)

1−8 All visitors fall in love with the chubby and endearing bottle trees (desert roses). They come in a range of shapes and colours, flaunting their pink flowers in February and March.

1, 2 & 3 Hilary Bradt, *4* Nicole Smoot; *5* Chris Miller, *6, 7 & 8* Hilary Bradt

11

Socotra also harbours a range of endemic plants, the names of which will be familiar to many gardeners, as related species are often grown in the horticulture trade. These include **hibiscus** (of which the endemic species have irritant hairs on their leaves – page 9), **Hypericum** (page 9), Pelargonium, **Geranium** (page 9), **Exacum** – the Persian violet – and, of course, *Begonia socotrana*. This latter was collected in 1880 by Isaac Bayley Balfour and cultivated at the Royal Botanic Garden Edinburgh. It is the only known **begonia** that is winter-flowering in nature and, as such, all winter-flowering begonias globally are in some way derived from this founding collection. Another begonia species is found only on a small cliff face on the tiny island of Samha – but this is not winter-flowering despite being closely related.

Local uses Many of the plants on Socotra are used by the Socotri people for a wide variety of purposes; in fact the inhabitants are very adept at finding a plant to fulfil a certain function. These uses are extensively documented in *Ethnoflora of the Soqotra Archipelago* (page 159) and over 750 of the species have at least one traditional use – those that do not are either extremely rare or were so poorly recorded that no information could be gained about them. Some of these endemic species are also well known outside the islands – for example **aloes** that have been harvested for their bitters, **frankincense** trees whose resin was traded in antiquity, and of course the **dragon's blood tree** which is the most iconic of all Socotri plants. The sap has a wide range of uses, including medicinal.

Frankincense is harvested from the genus *Boswellia*. There are only 24 species globally, with eleven species on Socotra – including *Boswellia samhaensis* on Samha Island, which was only described by researchers in 2020 – and as such Socotra is a centre of diversity for the genus (the remainder are in either northeast Africa, southern Arabia or the Indian subcontinent). Extensive woodlands can be seen in various parts of the island, and a series of species is found only on cliffs (page 14). They are an actively evolving group showing great variation, and are the focus of much research both historically and currently, as frankincense has become an extremely valuable commodity both in traditional markets and also in developing health, wellbeing and aromatherapy products. Many frankincense populations are globally under threat, and this could easily apply to species on Socotra should supplies start to run out elsewhere. The species on Socotra have been physically harvested, ie: they were never cut to induce resin production, but rather the resin was gathered from natural wounds and exudates. If this practice were to change then many of the species on Socotra would quickly become threatened through over-harvesting.

Some notable trees and flowers

1 *Euphorbia arbuscula* One of the most characteristic trees on Socotra. It is a key dry-season fodder for goats, and is also used as an insecticide. It has a particularly caustic latex, which is used for a variety of purposes including as an adhesive to stick together handwritten pages of the Qu'ran to make a small booklet.

2 *Punica protopunica* The only known relative of the cultivated pomegranate is endemic to Socotra. The fruits are small, rather bitter and caustic and therefore have little value as a food. However, the flowers can be turned upside down to ooze nectar, which was much prized in the days before sugar arrived on the islands.

3 *Exacum affine (Persian or Socotran violet)* Popular in the horticultural trade, it is not a violet at all – the common name derives from the colour and scent of its small flowers.

(Lisa Banfield)

(Lisa Banfield)

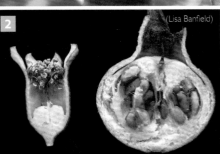
(Lisa Banfield)

(Hilary Bradt)

(Chris Miller)

(Lisa Banfield)

4 *Caralluma socotrana* Despite its name, this is not actually an endemic (it is also found in northeast Africa) but it is the showiest of the 30 or so species of the succulent asclepiads found on the island, with symmetrically jointed stems like green coral and deep crimson flowers.

5 *Boswellia bullata* Of the 24 species of frankincense tree worldwide, eleven are found on Socotra. *B. bullata* is found only on cliffs where they have evolved 'holdfasts' at the base of the trunk to cling to the sheer rock face.

FAUNA Compared with plants, and indeed the fauna of other remote islands, Socotra's fauna is less spectacular, but the high percentage of endemics in these small animals and birds makes them particularly interesting.

Invertebrates Bugs, beetles and other insects, as well as all the other creatures without backbones, constitute over 95% of the animals on earth, so it's not surprising that Socotra has its share of them (around 75% of the land fauna) with hundreds of endemic species – and no doubt many more to be discovered.

One interesting aspect of island evolution is the tendency of some insects, particularly beetles, to lose their ability to fly. Darwin speculated that, because islands are usually windy, some species give up the unequal struggle for purposeful flight and, with few predators around, remain grounded and gradually lose their wings. Given the intensity of the summer winds on Socotra, this seems a plausible explanation here. Socotra's 50 or so species of **grasshoppers**, all of which are endemic, include a wingless species, *Dioscoridus depressus*.

Land snails Snails do not rate highly in most travellers' interests, but some – giants and midgets – in Socotra will give them pause. Socotra has a total of 100 different land snail species, 98 of which are endemic. The giant, which will be found as empty shells on the arid plains, is *Riebeckia sokotorana*, whose conical, spiral shell can be 100mm long. Another endemic genus is *Balfouria* which is also conical but smaller and narrower. The midget isn't even obviously a snail – or hundreds of snails, when seen from a distance. And that's its protection. *Achatinelloides socotrensis* climbs up the trunks of large trees – often dragon's blood trees – during the dry season and packs together so tightly that, from a distance, they resemble a discolouration of the bark. The massing together reduces predation and also moisture loss, and provides some camouflage.

Moths and butterflies Moths evolved long before butterflies and were probably on Socotra when it was part of Gondwana. Butterflies, however, are a more recent evolutionary arrival and were most likely blown to the island from the mainland, evolving subspecies over time. Socotra has around 280 species of Lepidoptera, over 100 of which are endemic.

Visitors will only see moths during a night walk (their pin-prick red eyeshine is a give-away) but only experts will be able to identify the rather boring brownish moth their torch reveals. Butterflies, on the other hand, flutter cooperatively near at hand during walks so it's worth being able to give a name to the most obvious ones. Most visitors will see the largely white butterfly we conveniently, but of course erroneously, called a 'cabbage white'. It was actually *Belenois anomala,* an endemic subspecies of the caper white widely found in Africa and Asia. Likewise the swallowtail or citrus butterfly, *Papilio demodocus bennetti*, which aroused such passions among the Victorian collectors on Socotra (page 16). Perhaps the most attractive endemic that

1 **Scarlet darter** (Chris Miller)

2 **Male and female Socotra bluets**
(Kay Van Damme)

3 *Charaxes balfouri* (swift), an illustration
from *The Natural History of Sokotra and Abd-el-Kuri*
(page 159) (The Biodiversity Heritage Library)

4 **Socotra's colourful freshwater crabs are plentiful in the
wadi pools** (Chris Miller)

5 *A. socotrensis* **snails cluster together to deter predators
and retain moisture** (Hilary Bradt)

6 **Socotra Island blue baboon spider**
(Richard Porter)

15

All collectors are passionate about their subject, but perhaps few as fanatical as lepidopterists, especially those in the Victorian era. And especially when they've gone to the expense of going to a remote island to collect endemic butterflies. And when the scientific name of a rather beautiful butterfly carries the name of a 'dilettante sportsman' their scorn knows no bounds.

Over 100 years after Mr E N Bennett, a Fellow of Hertford College Oxford, journeyed to Socotra in 1886 with a butterfly net in his luggage, Kenneth Guichard commented that 'As an entomologist Bennett was barely worthy of the fine *papilio* named after him.' The butterfly in question was *Papilio demodocus bennetti*, a Socotran subspecies of the citrus butterfly, a swallowtail found in most parts of the world. Seventeen years later came the volatile collector W R Ogilvie Grant who, true to his era, felt that most challenges could be solved with a gun. Thus when he just missed netting a *bennetti* he lost his temper and shot it. Which rather defeated the purpose. Another time, reports Guichard, he was distracted by a Socotran sparrow which mobbed him just as he was closing in on an endemic butterfly. 'Greatly incensed by such an unprovoked attack I got my collecting gun and shot the offending bird.'

you are likely to see is the *Charaxes balfouri* or swift. This pretty butterfly is orange-brown with attractively patterned underwings. It is usually found above 500m, so look out for it on the walk up to Hoq Cave or Homhil.

Damselflies and dragonflies With the numerous rivers and streams in Socotra, it's not surprising that these beautiful insects are commonly seen and admired; most have close relatives in Africa and Arabia (page 18). The strikingly lovely red dragonfly is the common and widely distributed *Crocothemis erythraea* or scarlet darter. Only the males are red; the female is brown. Also see photo on page 15.

Arachnids: spiders and scorpions Socotra is home to some beautiful and very photogenic spiders (page 17), about half of which are endemic. None is as gorgeous as the Socotra Island **blue baboon spider**, *Monocentropus balfouri*, which hides in holes or crevices during the day so is hard to find, though photos abound since they are popular with the pet trade. Apart from Socotra, this genus occurs in two other places: Yemen and, surprisingly, Madagascar.

At the other end of the scale in terms of size and beauty is the **wolf spider**, a ground-living spider which we found in large numbers when going for a night walk near Diksam, where their yellow eyeshine made them easy to spot. We showed a photo to our guide who recoiled in horror. 'This is the most dangerous animal in Socotra!' He mimed the spider jumping on to his shoulder and then to his cheek. Spider expert Daniel Austin was more measured. 'This is a wolf spider (family Lycosidae). They do not build webs but rather stalk and hunt their prey on the ground. They're good mums, carrying their eggs around with them in a spherical silken bag and they continue to carry their spiderlings with them after birth, riding on the rear of their mother's abdomen. This looks fantastic in torchlight as wolf spiders give quite strong eyeshine, so a mum carrying babies looks like a shimmering gem! Can wolf spider venom harm a human? Not seriously, no, so I don't think your guide was right.'

1 TRICHONEPHILA SUMPTUOSA The rather magnificently named sumptuous golden orb-weaver is the largest of all the web-building spiders on Socotra. The 'golden' in its name refers not to the creature itself, but to the incredibly strong silk from which it spins its impressive web. The tiny spider in the top left of the photo is probably a male hoping to mate. When a spider's pedipalps (little leg-like structures in front of its face) look as though they are wearing boxing gloves, then it's a male. The boxing gloves are adapted for smearing sperm on the female's reproductive organs.

2 GASTERACANTHA SANGUINOLENTA At first glance looking for all the world like a minuscule crab, the female short-horn kite spider is strikingly red, yellow and black. Its unusual shape garnished with half a dozen spiky protrusions makes it rather more attractive than might be suggested by its scientific name, *Gasteracantha sanguinolenta*, which literally translates as 'bloody/gory thorny-back'.

3 ARGIOPE SECTOR From a distance, *Argiope* spiders often appear to have only four legs, as they rest in an unusual cross-shaped pose with their limbs in pairs. The centres of their webs are decorated with a zig-zag of white silk, which is known as a stabilimentum because it was originally thought to give stability to the structure. This explanation has since been dismissed but arachnologists continue to debate its true purpose: stabilimenta may help to camouflage the spider, make it appear larger, lure prey, or attract a mate – nobody is really sure. The current leading theory is that it highlights the presence of the web to birds, which might otherwise destroy it by flying through; but this protection comes at a cost, as it also tips off some potential prey to the trap, thereby reducing its effectiveness.

(Chris Miller)

(Chris Miller)

(Chris Miller)

Background Information   NATURAL HISTORY

1

A short rest at a beautiful sheltered wadi and its pools can be very welcome in Socotra. While you are there, why not take a brief look at some of the beautiful, unique freshwater fauna of the island?

There are many types of aquatic ecosystems here, from brackish water lagoons around Hadiboh and Qalansiyah, to wadi rock pools, streams and even underground lakes. Each of these ecosystems has its own typical birds, plants and invertebrates, besides some general species. Healthy freshwater environments on Socotra are important for humans and livestock, forming the island's primary drinking water resources. Water quality is sensitive to human impacts – a great diversity of species in combination with clear water are useful general indicators of healthy streams. Several unique freshwater species on Socotra are included in the IUCN Red List.

The most striking species you can encounter when visiting a wadi here are the colourful **damsel-** and **dragonflies**. The dragonflies are the larger, often hovering, species that cannot fold their wings over their bodies; the damselflies are the slender smaller ones that can fold their wings over their backs. You can spot bright red or blue dragonflies perching at most places with surface water on the island, including the brackish coastal lagoons. A total of 22 species of dragonflies have been recorded from the island, but one is now extinct.

In the **Socotri language**, dragonflies are generally named *'idbihir di-rīho* or *'the buzzing flying insect of freshwater'* (*rīho* means 'water'), recognising them as a sign of good water. They have evocative names in English, such as the broad scarlet, the red-veined dropwing or the epaulet skimmer. One species that can be seen in the mountains and plateaux of eastern Socotra occurs nowhere else in

Lift any stone in Socotra and you're likely to find a **scorpion**. The island has five species, four of which are endemic. These arachnids have changed little for 350 million years, being perfectly suited to a variety of habitats including desert since they have no need to drink, deriving all the moisture they need from their prey. Needless to say, you should not try to handle one.

Crustaceans Few visitors leave the island without a '**lobster**' treat. These are not true lobsters with claws but spiny lobsters or crayfish. Either way, they're delicious and seem plentiful in the warm seas around Socotra.

Freshwater **crabs** are something of a feature of Socotra's mountain streams – see opposite. One conspicuous salt-water crab is the comical **ghost crab** – almost white with extra-long eye-stalks and one claw larger than the other – which are found on tropical and sub-tropical beaches throughout the world. *Ocypode ceratophthalmus* dig deep burrows in the sand which end in a chamber, and heap the excavated sand into towers to advertise their presence to potential mates or rivals. They are remarkably fleet of foot and often only glimpsed out of the corner of your eye, scurrying to their burrows. Largely nocturnal, they emerge at night to feed.

Reptiles Much of this section has been provided by Raquel Vasconcelos (page vii)
Around 90% of the island's reptiles are endemic. Half of these are geckos, and all visitors will see the **Socotra rock gecko** (*Pristurus sokotranus*) sunning itself by a path. They are sometimes known as semaphore geckos, because of their comical 'push ups' when confronted by a predator or territorial competitor, including a

the world: the **Socotra bluet** (*Azuragrion granti*). This slender, beautiful damselfly can often be seen flying in tandem (male and female together) and can be quite abundant in slow-running streams. It is an indicator of clear water and is very sensitive to pollution. These bluets are not at all camera-shy, so you can get a good souvenir photo.

Another striking freshwater species, unique to the island, is the brightly coloured **Socotra freshwater crab**. Mostly these beautiful creatures are hiding under boulders in the water. If you remain patient, you may spot them slowly coming out from under the stones and crossing a wadi pool or a stream. Brightly orange, yellow, or even purple in colour, these crabs are very conspicuous. The endemic species (and genus) *Socotrapotamon socotrensis* is quite special because it has no relatives in Arabia or Africa, but shows connections towards eastern Asia – they are considered ancient relicts of which the ancestors were most likely present in the island before its separation from southern Arabia. The crabs are not edible, and as scavengers and hunters they fulfil an important function. If you are crossing a wadi on foot, please take care not to step on one: the crab won't enjoy it and nor will your toes.

If you see a very abundant **small fish** (Arabian toothcarp) in some freshwater wadis, and some larger **conical molluscs** (red-rimmed melania), these do not belong in Socotra. They are **invasive species** and they may threaten the existence of the native, endemic species.

An information leaflet with photos and text about Socotra's aquatic animals is available in Arabic (for your guide) and English on the Friends of Soqotra website, w friendsofsoqotra.org.

potential mate. Also frequently seen is the **Socotra skink** (*Trachylepis socotrana*) with its iridescent brown skin, but the other 29 terrestrial species of reptile are harder to find. A special discovery, for most people, is the **Socotran chameleon** (*Chamaeleo monachus*) which is relatively common at higher altitudes (Chris Miller found several on his camel trek; page 120), but much easier to spot at night when they turn a lighter colour so the famous camouflage is less effective. Talking of camouflage, it's an oft-quoted myth that chameleons can change their colour to blend with the background. Most chameleon species do indeed change colour, but this is much more to do with emotion. That said, the Socotran chameleon does seem to have a greater range of colours than usual, varying from brown to green, according to sex, probably, and to its mood – including stress at being discovered, when it can become aggressive. For this reason, it is often known as the hissing chameleon although this response, along with an open mouth and inflated throat, is not unusual in chameleons. This endemic species has relatives in Asia and Africa and is thought to be the oldest in its group, having diverged from the others 10–15 million years ago. Note that more recently, as tourism numbers have increased, you may occasionally see children holding chameleons up on sticks at the side of roads in rural areas. Please don't encourage this and resist the urge to stop for a photo; the chameleons need to spend their days hunting rather than used as bait for your tourist dollars.

Two other hard-to-find lizards – but thrilling if you succeed – are the **dragon's blood tree gecko** (*Hemidactylus dracaenacolus*) which lives, as you might guess, exclusively in the canopy and in holes in the trunk of the dragon's blood tree (*Dracaena*

1 & 3 The Socotra chameleon is mostly found at higher altitudes. The single species demonstrates a range of colours, from green to brown, according to mood and environment (1 Chris Miller, 3 Richard Porter)

2 Socotra rock gecko (Chris Miller)

4 Günther's racer snake. This is the commonest of Socotra's two harmless racer snakes and can be recognised by the vertical pupil, which is similar to that of a viper (Raquel Vasconcelos)

5 Socotra skink (Raquel Vasconcelos)

6 *Haemodracon riebeckii*, an endemic species of gecko (Raquel Vasconcelos)

cinnabari), and the **giant Socotra gecko** (*Haemodracon riebeckii*), an endemic genus and a relative monster at 20cm long. It also lives in these trees but more often in rock crevices and boulders. Both species are, however, nocturnal so seldom seen unless you are fortunate enough to be camped near a forest of *D. cinnabari*.

Of the two species of racer **snake** that you might come across, the most common is Günther's racer (*Ditypophis vivax*). This snake looks very similar to a viper and probably plays an important role in controlling (introduced) rodents. Easily recognised, despite its colour variation, is the Socotran racer snake (*Hemerophis socotrae*), which varies in colour from yellow, red or brown, or banded with black. Both species are the only one in their genus and probably relics from a Gondwana heritage. They are now extinct on the mainland.

All snakes – and indeed all reptiles – on Socotra are harmless and beneficial to the ecology of the island, although many Socotri fear them.

Birds   *This section has been written by Richard Porter*

A total of over 220 species of birds have been recorded in the Socotra archipelago. Of the 42 that breed regularly, the Jouanin's petrel (*Bulweria fallax*) and Socotra bunting (*Emberiza socotrana*) are considered near-threatened, while the Egyptian vulture (*Neophron percnopterus*), Socotra buzzard (*Buteo socotraensis*), Abd el Kuri sparrow (*Passer hemileucus*) and Socotra cormorant (*Phalacrocorax nigrogularis*) are globally threatened species. These are the islands' top priority for protection and conservation.

While the Egyptian vulture is globally endangered, Socotra probably holds the highest concentration of this species in the world with a population of nearly 2,000. This is the most familiar bird on the island, circling over the towns and villages and coming to feed on household scraps and leftovers from a restaurant meal. On your journey from the airport to Hadiboh you might easily count 50. Highly respected by the Socotri, it is nicknamed 'municipal bird' for its role in refuse disposal and often features in their folklore and poetry.

Many birds encountered on Socotra are migrants, most stopping off on their long journey to and from their breeding grounds in Europe and Asia and their wintering areas in Africa. These total over 175 species of which only about 70 occur regularly; the rest are very rare. Probably the most colourful migrant is the blue-cheeked bee-eater (*Merops persicus*), which can suddenly arrive on the island in large numbers, while one of the most frequently seen is the desert wheatear (*Oenanthe deserti*); many will have travelled all the way from China to spend the winter on Socotra. In 2019 a common cuckoo (*Cuculus canorus*) was tracked by satellite all the way from

WHICH STARLING IS THAT?   *Richard Porter*

There are two starlings in Socotra, both with bright orange patches in the wing: the common Somali starling and the rarer, endemic Socotra starling. The Somali starling is found throughout the island and you will often see flocks flying over Hadiboh. They are highly vocal and you will be attracted to them by their loud whistling calls as they pass overhead. The Socotra starling lives mainly in the highlands and is more difficult to find.

The Somali starling is slightly larger with a long, graduated tail. Apart from the orange wing-patches the male is glossy black, but the female has a grey head. In the smaller, shorter-tailed Socotra starling, both sexes are glossy black with orange wing-patches.

1 Socotra white-eye (Richard Porter)

2 Socotra warbler (Richard Porter)

3 Socotra sunbird (Richard Porter)

4 Socotra sparrow (Richard Porter)

5 Socotra scops owl (Richard Porter)

6   Socotra golden-winged grosbeak
    (Richard Porter)

7   Socotra buzzard (Richard Porter)

8   Socotra bunting (Richard Porter)

9   Socotra starling (Richard Porter)

10 Socotra cisticola (Richard Porter)

1 Sooty gulls (Chris Miller)

2 Brown booby *(left)* and Socotra cormorant *(right)*
  (Chris Miller)

3 Lesser crested terns (Chris Miller)

4 Black-winged stilt (Richard Porter)

5 Masked booby (Richard Porter)

6 Jouanin's petrel (SS)

7 Egyptian vulture (Chris Miller)

8 Long-billed pipit (Chris Miller)

9 Laughing dove (Chris Miller)

10 Blue-cheeked bee-eater (Richard Porter)

11 Female Somali starling (Richard Porter)

Richard Porter

In June 2019, a team of international ornithologists visited Khurkh in northeastern Mongolia to fit satellite transmitters to five cuckoos to track their migration. A key part of the Mongolian Cuckoo Project was visiting local schools to raise awareness about migratory birds and invite the students to give names to the cuckoos. The transmitter signals later indicated that three of the cuckoos reached Africa, all crossing the Arabian Sea and two the Saudi Arabian desert. In November, one of the cuckoos named Namjaa (Mongolian for 'storyteller') briefly stopped on Socotra, a very important place for migratory birds crossing the Arabian Sea to rest and feed on their long journeys to Africa.

Learning that Namjaa had visited Socotra, schoolchildren in Mongolia decided to write to their counterparts on the island to thank them for the safe passage of 'their' cuckoos and tell them how important their island is, not only for its resident birds but also for the countless migratory birds that cross the Arabian Sea on their intercontinental journeys.

A delightful exchange of letters followed, including these:

From Mongolia:

Hello my friends. My name is Shinekhuu. I live in the countryside and was born in a herder family. When I was a child, cuckoos used to sing almost every morning. But I have never seen a cuckoo! One day, researchers who study cuckoos visited us and told a lot about cuckoos and their migration. I'm so glad to hear that the three cuckoos we named have crossed the ocean and an island and then finally reached their wintering destination. I could not imagine how those birds travelled 13,000km. I really want this bird to return to Mongolia. You should please take care of the birds and wildlife on the island of Socotra.

Dear Socotran school friends. I am Semuun. There are many species of birds and animals in Mongolia. I and my classmates are very pleased to give the name to the cuckoo that has come a long way to East Africa. I have heard that the island where you live is an important place for thousands of birds. I am writing a letter for the first time to my friends abroad. Good luck with your work and everything.

A few days later the Socotri school children penned their replies, including these:

My name is Ashraf Saeed. I am studying in the second year at Khaled Ibn Al Waleed High School. Thank you for writing to us, we are amazed by the small bird Namjaa travelling such long distances. We hope Namjaa will return safely. I wish you can manage to visit Socotra one day and see its rare bird and plant species. Below is one of the interesting birds, Egyptian Vulture, called locally 'Su'aidoo'. [A very accomplished drawing of an Egyptian vulture followed]

My Name is Yu'adah. I am in the first year at Al Zahra'a Secondary School for girls in Socotra How are you? I thank you for your letters to us. We are proud of the bird Namjaa who visited us and we hope Namjaa will come back and fly over Socotra on his way home to Mongolia. We hope you can visit Socotra and see all kinds of birds and animals and landscape.

So children of two remote parts of the world, brought together by one migrating bird!·

Mongolia to Africa, stopping on Socotra on the way. This caused much excitement, especially among school children in both Mongolia and Socotra who sent lovely messages to each other about the importance of birds (see opposite).

Detailed studies have determined the populations and mapped the distributions of all Socotra's breeding species. These have shown the five commonest land birds to be the Socotra sparrow (*Passer insularis*), black-crowned sparrow-lark (*Eremopterix nicriceps*), laughing dove (*Spilopelia senegalensis*), Somali starling (*Onychogathus blythii*) and long-billed pipit (*Anthus similis*). All will soon become familiar birds to the enquiring tourist.

However, it is the twelve **endemic species** that the visiting birdwatcher will most want to see: the Socotra buzzard (*Buteo socotraensis*), Socotra scops owl (*Otus socotranus*), Socotra sunbird (*Chalcomitra balfouri*) – an important pollinator of the island's flowers, Socotra warbler (*Incana incana*), Socotra cisticola (*Cisticola haesitatus*), Socotra starling (*Onychogathus frater*) – but note this is very similar to the non-endemic Somali starling (page 21), Socotra golden-winged grosbeak (*Rhynchostruthus socotranus*), Socotra sparrow (*Passer insularis*), Abd el Kuri sparrow (*Passer hemileucus*), Socotra white-eye (*Zosterops socotranus*), Socotra bunting (*Emberiza socotrana*), and Jouanin's petrel (*Bulweria fallax*).

Along with its Arabian mainland cousin, the golden-winged grosbeak is Yemen's **national bird**.

Most of the endemics can be easily seen, but there are three exceptions. Without special effort, the owl will only be heard, the Socotri likening its night-time monotonous, rhythmical song to the chanting of a prayer. For the Abd el Kuri sparrow you will have to take a long boat trip to the island of Abd el Kuri (off-limits to tourists at the time of writing; page 154), while the bunting, with its humbug-striped head, can only be found in the more remote parts of the mountains and hills and you'll need a good local guide, or a lot of luck, to find one.

Along the shores and in the wadi estuaries a variety of **migrant ducks, wading birds, gulls** and **terns** can easily be observed. Look for black-winged stilts (*Himantopus himantopus*) on their long, pink legs, sooty gulls (*Ichthyaetus hemprichii*) and flocks of lesser crested terns (*Thalasseus bengalensis*) resting during their annual migration.

While on boat trips or walking along the shore and looking out to sea you may spot a feeding flock of Socotra cormorants (*Phalacrocorax nigrogularis*), a brown booby (*Sula leucogaster*) diving headlong for fish from several metres above the waves, or even a masked booby (*Sula dactylatra*). These seabirds breed on Socotra's remote islands and rocky outcrops along with other marine birds and these large colonies are of international importance. Despite its name, the Socotra cormorant is not, in fact, an endemic to Socotra, though it does breed on the island. Socotra was simply the place it was first discovered, described and named. The largest numbers nest in the Arabian Gulf.

If you are very lucky, or take a boat trip out to sea, you may just spot a Jouanin's petrel (*Bulweria fallax*), an all-black, long-winged seabird whose first nest discovered in the world was found on Socotra in 2000. Until then its breeding grounds had been a mystery.

The birds of the Socotra archipelago have been the subject of many taxonomic studies in recent years. These have included the identification and naming of the resident buzzard as *Buteo socotraensis* in 2010 – which led to *Guinness Book of Records* listing it as the 'most recently discovered bird of prey species' in the world.

For a complete checklist of the all the birds of Socotra, with some photos, visit w osme.org/2020/04/checklist-of-the-birds-of-the-socotra-archipelago.

1–4 There are no endemic mammals on Socotra and the only wild mammals are (introduced) civets and bats, with the lesser mouse-tailed bat easily seen at Dagub Cave. Domestic animals include cows, camels and goats — all of which have adapted to their new environment.

1 & 2 Chris Miller, *3* Hilary Bradt,
4 Chris Miller

Mammals Although Socotra separated from the mainland after the evolution of mammals, there are (probably) no endemic species on the island. (A tiny shrew is thought – possibly – to be endemic.) Four species of bat, however, have found the numerous caves to their liking, the most common being the **lesser mouse-tailed bat** (*Rhinopoma hardwickii*) which may be seen at the back of Dagub Cave and is easily identified by its long tail. A species of the trident bat, *Asellia italosomalica*, is also present and is smaller than its Somali relative, so may be an endemic subspecies.

The lack of native animals is more than made up by the introduced ones, particularly **goats** which were introduced before the 13th century and now roam the island in huge numbers. Some visitors regard them with fascination, some with revulsion, but there is no doubt that they serve a valuable purpose, eating almost anything, including plastic, so doing their part in clearing up the rubbish in Hadiboh, and also providing the locals with milk, meat and hair with which to make ropes.

Less plentiful domestic animals are the cattle, sheep and camels, all of which have developed Socotri characteristics. The **cattle** and **sheep** are smaller than elsewhere and the **camels** (dromedaries; page 119) are exceptionally sure-footed on the rocky terrain, as will be noted with relief by all who do a camel trek.

A more surprising introduction is the lesser Indian **civet**, which resembles a cat but belongs in the mongoose family. In the past these were highly valued for their contribution to the perfume trade – they secrete a musk from a gland below their tail. Shakespeare is referring to the civet when King Lear says 'Thou owest the worm no silk, the beast no hide, the sheep no wool, the cat no perfume.' On Socotra civets are still occasionally trapped to extract the musk but are mostly regarded as a nuisance since they steal dates, which were vital to a family's survival.

As on all islands, there are plenty of accidentally introduced mice and rats. Indeed, the latter are so large and bold around human habitation that Hadiboh has sometimes been dubbed Ratiboh. Cats have been introduced to deal with this problem, but there are no dogs on the island.

Marine life Socotra, being at the meeting point of the Arabian Sea and the Indian Ocean, is particularly rich in marine life – there are over 730 species of fish, for instance, far too many to describe here. So what follows is just a brief overview with some of the more exciting species to look out for.

Visitors who go to Rosh and Dihamri marine nature sanctuaries in the north will find the beaches literally carpeted with fragments of coral, shells and other dead marine creatures washed up by the tides. The island's coral reefs are tiny, only 2km² in size, but they are largely unexploited and don't seem prone to coral bleaching so are rewarding for snorkellers and scuba divers (page 55) if the weather is favourable.

In former days the island has attracted sports fishermen for the marlin, barracuda, tuna and travelly, and there are also several species of shark. In *Socotra: A Natural History* there is a description of the diet of one species: 'Tiger sharks will eat almost anything including other sharks, sheep, birds, tyres and sealed bottles of mayonnaise.' Perhaps tourists, too.

These predators are rarely seen, however. Marine mammals are more likely to be spotted, particularly the spinner dolphins which cavort around your boat en route to Shu'ab beach. Five other species of dolphin have been reported around the island, and occasionally killer whales are seen. Sperm whale casualties have left their huge skeletal remains around Ras Erissel and the south. The shallow waters of lagoons, most notably Detwah which is on everyone's itinerary, are extraordinarily rich in very visible marine life due to the sea grass which provides protection and food for a variety of creatures: puffer fish, cuttlefish, octopus, stingrays and crabs.

1

2

3

4

1 Spinner dolphins can frequently be seen on boat trips between Qalansiyah and Shu'ab (Nicole Smoot)

2 Yellowtail tang swimming among coral (Sergey Strelkov/D)

3 Whale sharks are one of several shark species found around Socotra (Chris Miller)

4 Loggerhead turtles nest on Socotra's north coast (Natursports/S)

5 Shoreline procession (sanderlings and ghost crab) (Chris Miller)

5

During the late 1990s there were several large-scale international projects on Socotra, primarily designed to record and recognise the unique natural heritage of the islands and to conserve them for the future. As a result, Socotra became well known internationally for the amazing and unique species and habitats that occur there. One of the major results of these projects was discussions between international, national and local partners that resulted in the Socotra Conservation Zoning Plan (SCZP), adopted by Presidential Decree 275 in the year 2000. It was designed through extensive community consultations to recommend guidelines for the sustainable use and conservation of the unique biodiversity of the archipelago, both terrestrial and marine; and to have 'Nature Sanctuaries' where very little activity would be permitted, in order to conserve biodiversity and evolution in situ.

The 'National Park' – which covers approximately 70% of the main island of Socotra and all outlying islands – has a range of activities that are prohibited, whereas the 'Resource Use Zone' has some permitted activities. The two major towns and their immediate environs – the capital Hadiboh, and Qalansiyah in the west – are designated 'General Use Zones' where development is already advanced and expanding. The marine plan followed a similar logic, with areas important for the ecological integrity of Socotra's marine systems designated as Nature Sanctuaries.

It is widely acknowledged that the SCZP now requires updating, to address new methods, better community involvement and management planning as well as to include cultural features. Certainly, some restricted activities have still been taking place, largely because of a lack of understanding and collaboration between responsible authorities. One example has been extensive road building, in parts of the National Park and across heritage locations, that has been detrimental to the integrity of the landscape. There is also a lack of enforcement capability, which means that investors planning to build private residences or visitor infrastructure can do so (almost) with impunity.

(See also *Appendix 3* on page 163, which includes a map of the terrestrial zones.)

Loggerhead turtles come ashore between May and September to lay their eggs on the sandy beaches of the north coast. Green turtles breed on Abd el Kuri, and hawksbill and olive ridleys are sometimes seen but are not known to breed on the islands.

For more information about the protection of vulnerable marine areas, see pages 92 and 163.

HISTORY

Just like its landscapes, Socotra's history is more varied than the island's size might suggest, from tales of serpents, spices and sorcery to British India's attempt in 1834 to buy it as a coaling stop for British steamships.

PREHISTORY AND LEGEND The island's first inhabitants date back to prehistoric times, and left archaeologically valuable traces of their presence on rocks and in caves (pages 34, 86 and 108). Many known or potential sites await further investigation and should yield important data, particularly the island's extensive cave network, much of which is still largely unexplored. Whether these unknown voyagers sailed their small craft deliberately to the island or were blown off course and shipwrecked on its shores, their new home offered them fresh water, caves for shelter, an abundance of seafood and the absence of fierce animals.

Those early inhabitants left proof of their existence, but much unverifiable legend followed. Did Socotra inspire the writer of the ancient epic *Gilgamesh*, in the second millennium BC, to feature it as the place where Gilgamesh dived to grasp the 'small spiny bush that grows in the waters of the Great Deep' (Stephen Mitchell's translation) that bore the secret of eternal youth, only to have it stolen from him by a serpent? Is it the *Pa-anch* mentioned in an Egyptian tale of around 1800BC, where a shipwrecked nobleman found medicinal and edible plants (and many serpents)? Did Alexander the Great, in the fourth century BC, send Greeks to Socotra to cultivate supplies of aloe? Was St Thomas the Apostle shipwrecked there on his way to India (AD52) and did he use his enforced visit to establish Christianity on the island? We don't know, but the conjecture adds to its mystique and appeal.

RECORDS BEGIN The *Pa-anch* (or Panchaia) connection cropped up again in other forms, as did possible references to Socotra under different names. Certainly the Egyptians were seeking sources of myrrh, frankincense and other fragrant or medicinal plants, and it seems highly likely they traded with Socotra, as did the early Greeks. By around the second century BC settlers from the Indian sub-continent were living there with the native inhabitants, later to be joined by Greeks and then Arabs. By the final century BC, the island was an important player in the incense trade: in the *Periplus of the Erythraean Sea*, a seafaring manual written in the first century AD that describes navigation and trading opportunities in the area, Socotra was mentioned (under the Greek name Dioscorida, which Pliny the Elder had also used) as having *'rivers in it and crocodiles and many snakes and great lizards of which the flesh is eaten and the fat melted and used instead of olive oil'*. (In

THE GOLD OF THE EAST

The Bible demonstrates the high value placed on Socotra's natural products in ancient times, with the Magi offering their gifts of gold, frankincense and myrrh – the latter two as costly as the gold. The medicinal sap of the Socotran aloe and pigment from the dragon's blood tree were also greatly prized. As its name implies, *Dracaena cinnabari*'s 'blood' could be used as a substitute for cinnabar, a dangerously toxic mineral produced by volcanic activity and used as a pigment for paint or lacquer. Dragon's blood, on the other hand, was harmless, so safe for a much wider variety of uses including cosmetics and medicine. The Romans smeared it on gladiators, as both decoration and a disinfectant (less glamorously it's said to be a cure for haemorrhoids). It was also employed later in the finishing stages of violin making; Stradivarius himself is thought to have used dragon's blood lacquer. Little wonder then that one possible origin (among many) suggested for the island's name is the Arabic *Suq-qutra* which translates as 'emporium of resin'. Frankincense too was much prized and in high demand, notably for burning during religious and other ceremonies; apparently at the funeral of Nero's wife an entire year's harvest literally went up in flames.

fact there's no record that large reptiles ever existed there.) The island is described as *'subject to the king of the Frankincense country'* and as carrying out trade with the Indian sub-continent; it is thought to have been cultivating large quantities of dragon's blood trees, frankincense and aloe and in fact trading throughout the Indian Ocean, India, Africa, Arabia and the Mediterranean. Diodorus of Sicily wrote at the time that it 'supplied the whole world' with myrrh and its frankincense perfumed the bath-houses of Rome.

THE MIDDLE AGES A long period of relatively uneventful trading history followed, with occasional reports from visitors. Christianity was introduced (whether by St Thomas or later by the Greeks) and survived until at least the 13th century, when Marco Polo reported that the island's inhabitants were baptised Christians with an archbishop who was answerable to an archbishop in Baghdad. He also reported that the island was a haunt of pirates, and that its women were well versed in sorcery: other tales have them making the island disappear, summoning up a storm at sea if invaders threatened, or, siren-like, luring sailors to shipwreck on the rocky coast.

From the 15th century the island was under mainland Arab control, apart from a brief four-year rule by Portugal from 1507 (page 85), and Christianity slowly gave way to Islam. The British visited in the 17th century, seeking a source of aloe, but then found more accessible provision elsewhere. A mixed population of African, Indian, Greek and Arabian origins lived mainly around the coast, while the earlier inhabitants led a largely pastoral life in the central highlands and plains.

A suggestion that, when Shakespeare wrote *The Tempest* in 1610–11, Prospero's island was inspired by Socotra is as unsubstantiated as it is imaginative. Although… there was active trade and shipping in the surrounding seas at the time, and who knows whether, in one of London's internationally frequented taverns, the bard may have encountered some merchant or old seadog who told him tales…

….the isle is full of noises,
Sounds and sweet airs, that give delight and hurt not.
Sometimes a thousand twangling instruments
Will hum about mine ears, and sometime voices
That, if I then had waked after long sleep,
Will make me sleep again…

It may also not be a coincidence that Shakespeare's friend and patron, the Earl of Southampton, had joined the East India Company (whose voyages included Socotra) in 1609.

THE 19TH CENTURY In 1834 Britain was back on the scene. After a survey and detailed report of the island by the enthusiastic Lieutenant James Wellsted of the East India Company's Marine Service, the government of British India sent a request to the island's rulers – the Sultans of Fartak and Qishn on the Arabian mainland – to purchase the island as a coaling station for British ships, and they agreed. In October, Acting Commander Haines of the Indian navy was sent from Bombay with the sum of 10,000 dollars to hand over in payment; however, Socotra's local ruler, Sheik Omer Abn Tuari, retorted (in effect) that even for a roomful of gold the British should not have an island which for many ages had been his fathers' heritage, so the deal was called off. The Sultan did, some years later, reconsider and re-open negotiations; but in 1839 the British captured Aden whose harbour was more suitable. The completion of the Suez Canal in 1869 shaved 7,000 miles

1 The campsite of the Forbes Expedition in 1898 at Adho Demelah, where these days the camel trekkers spend the night (National Museums Liverpool)

2 Ancient rock art, such as at Dahaisi Cave, provides evidence of Socotra's prehistoric inhabitants (Chris Miller)

3 The rusty old Soviet tanks that you'll sometimes see along the coast are relics from the 1980s, when the USSR supported South Yemen's communist movement (Chris Miller)

off the journey between Britain and India, which increased Britain's interest. In 1876 the Sultan of Qishn agreed that for an annual fee Socotra would never be ceded to anyone other than the British, and in 1886 the archipelago (and the Mahra Sultanate of Qishn on the mainland, to which it still belonged) became part of Britain's **Aden Protectorate**. The Sultan maintained his authority, and moved his residence to the island.

The islanders received little from their 'protectors' beyond occasional shipments of food or medical supplies, and their life was hard, whereas science benefited to varying extents from the number of surveys carried out on the island: zoological, botanical, geological, anthropological, linguistic and archaeological. Professor Isaac Bayley Balfour's comprehensive botanical survey in 1880 yielded descriptions of more than 200 plant species new to science; he later became Regius Keeper of Edinburgh's Royal Botanic Garden (RBGE), thus creating the relationship between the RBGE and Socotra that still continues today (page 7). He and others felt that much more could be discovered from further expeditions; and Socotra was firmly on the bucket list of Henry Ogg Forbes, a Scottish explorer, ornithologist and botanist who was then director and ornithologist at the Liverpool Museums. Forbes secured funding and in 1898 a joint expedition of the British and Liverpool museums set off, focused primarily on zoological collecting. The eleven-man team providently included the Liverpool Museum's taxidermist, and in addition took 'interpreters, cooks, gun carriers and personal guards'. They stayed on the islands for almost 11 weeks, returning with many specimens. Today World Museum, National Museums Liverpool (the successor to the Liverpool Museums), has considerable information related to the expedition and holds occasional exhibitions about Socotra.

TO THE PRESENT DAY Socotra remained part of the Protectorate until 1967; during World War II the RAF had a military base on the island which saw active service as a launch pad for strikes against German and Japanese submarines. A 1954 report gives the main export as ghee (clarified butter) which went to Bombay, Arabia and Zanzibar. Lesser ones were aloe, some frankincense, and the secretion from civets used as an ingredient in perfumery. Of a population estimated at 6,000–8,000 about half were a mixture of incomers (mainly of Arab and African origin) living around the coast, while the original inhabitants (known as **Bedouin**) still lived and cared for their livestock in the highlands and central plateaux. In 1944, they were estimated to have about 17,000 cows, sheep and goats, and 800 camels. Today – as visitors cannot fail to notice – the goats predominate.

In November 1967 mainland politics intervened dramatically: a detachment of the Yemen National Front landed on Socotra, the Sultanate of Mahra and Socotra was abolished, and Socotra became a region within the newly proclaimed **Independent People's Republic of Yemen** which used it as 'a military zone of restricted access'. The old Soviet tanks that you'll see rusting to death on some parts of the coast date from the 1980s, when the USSR was supporting South Yemen's communist movement.

Unification of the country in 1990 created the all-encompassing **Republic of Yemen** but, as we know, did not bring peace, although to Socotra's benefit the government did express interest in conserving its valuable biodiversity and cultural heritage. In 1997 the UNDP Socotra Biodiversity Project was set up, becoming the broader Socotra Conservation and Development Programme in 2001; and in 2003 UNESCO designated the archipelago a Man and the Biosphere Reserve and then, in 2008, a **World Heritage Site**, because of its exceptionally rich and distinct flora and fauna and high rate of endemic species. In 2013 Socotra, which since 1990 had been under first the administration of Sana'a, next that of Aden and then that of the

Hadhramawt Governorate, was given its own independent administrative identity, as **Socotra Governorate**, answerable to the UN-recognised Yemeni government on the mainland but with its Governor resident on the island. The beginnings of tourism were also – somewhat erratically – under way, although initially there had been some hesitation because of the potential threat to the archipelago's precious natural heritage.

However, by 2014 Yemen's long-running political turbulence was escalating into today's appalling war and in 2015 Socotra was devastated by cyclones Chapala and Megh, which caused massive damage to homes, livelihoods (including tourism) and natural assets from which the islands have still not fully recovered. Although less severe than Megh, cyclone Mukunu (in 2018) brought further destruction.

In 2024, Socotra is buffeted by international politics. Its position on main shipping lanes makes it a strategically desirable base for ambitious neighbouring powers, while Yemen, drained by ongoing violence, offers little support. The UAE and Saudi Arabia have given generous humanitarian and financial aid, both having invested in infrastructure projects in Socotra building roads, houses, hospitals, schools and even football stadiums, but their increased profile on the island risks displacing Socotra's own unique and very special character and traditions. Once lost, they cannot be recreated. In June 2020 the UAE-backed Southern Transitional Council ousted the island's Yemeni administration in a bloodless coup, with Saudi Arabia turning a blind eye. Troops, weapons and other equipment have arrived from the mainland, and there are now several military posts on Socotra. Satellite photos also show ongoing construction activity on Abd el Kuri, including the building of a large runway, rumoured to be a UAE military base. While uncertain, this may well explain why tourists were prohibited from visiting the outer islands as of late 2023.

International awareness and concern for Socotra are growing now: its amazing natural heritage belongs to the world, and not to individual powers. Given its uniqueness and the resilience of its people there is still hope; but, as we write this, the future looks far from secure.

CULTURE AND PEOPLE

We are grateful to our invaluable specialist contributors – pages vi and vii – for several pieces in this section.

Socotra's population has over the ages divided geographically and culturally into two groups of people: those living in the highlands who belong to kin-based tribal groups, own land, and have access to specific land and water resources; and those (mostly African and Arab settlers) who live along the coastal plains, have no tribal affiliation and do not own land. The highlanders call themselves 'Bedouin', but not in (for example) the Sahara-Desert sense of nomads with no fixed home who wander long distances with their animals; these live permanently in the mountainous interior and their 'transhumance' consists of shifting their herds from pasture to pasture there.

LANGUAGE AND POETRY *Miranda Morris*

> Linguistic diversity is the store of knowledge about how to maintain and use sustainably some of the most diverse, but also most vulnerable, environments. With the death of each language, this knowledge dies too.
>
> The UNESCO Endangered Languages Program website

There are three inhabited islands in the Socotra archipelago: Socotra, Samha and Abd el Kuri. They share a unique language and culture. Socotri is one of the six Modern South Arabian Languages (MSAL), unwritten Semitic languages spoken by minority populations in southeast Yemen, southern Oman and the fringes of southeast Saudi Arabia. The name 'Modern South Arabian' is somewhat confusing, as these unwritten languages are neither 'modern' nor comprehensible to an Arabic speaker: they are called 'Modern South Arabian Languages' (MSAL) to differentiate them from 'Old South Arabian' which refers to the four related languages which were written in the Ancient South Arabian script and are now extinct. The MSAL are believed to be the remnants of a pre-Arabic substratum that once stretched over the whole of southern Arabia and across the Red Sea into the highlands and littoral of East Africa. The areas in which the MSAL are still spoken are the only regions within the Arabian Peninsula to have retained the Semitic languages spoken prior to the spread of Islam and subsequent Arabisation of the peninsula. In all other communities Arabic appears to have superseded the original languages.

As a result of the spread of Arabic among MSAL speakers, caused by rapid economic and socio-political change in recent decades, these languages are increasingly falling into disuse. In both Oman and Yemen today, the official language is Arabic: of education, government, the media and commerce. Being in competition with another more widely spoken and literate language is a common problem for purely oral languages. However, in the case of the MSAL, the official language in question is Arabic. As this is also the language of the Qu'ran, and one which Muslims (nearly a quarter of the world's population) work hard to learn, it means that these six minority languages are in competition with an extremely high-prestige language. Today, the vast majority of MSAL speakers speak Arabic as well as their own language.

As is the case in many oral cultures, Socotri has an extremely rich poetic tradition, which as well as poems also includes prayers, lullabies, work chants, community wisdom enshrined in poetic couplets, messages in code, riddles, and stories centred on a short poem or exchange of poems. This valuable and irreplaceable repository of linguistic and ethnographic material is decaying even more rapidly than the language

1 One of various traditional fishing methods (Chris Miller)

2 A typical fishing hamlet. The rough coastal terrain in some areas can hamper communication between neighbouring settlements (Simon Urwin)

3 Harvesting the sap of aloes, which is collected in a pot beneath the cut ends. The rocks hold the leaves in place (Soqotra Heritage Project)

4 A coastal saltern. Sea water is left to evaporate creating a thick brine which is collected and dried to make salt – this traditional occupation continues on a small scale today (Soqotra Heritage Project)

5 Preparing the catch of the day, Qalansiyah (Simon Urwin)

1 A welcome sight! An ice cream seller, Ras Erissel (Nicole Smoot)

2 A healthy drink of milk from a locally made vessel (Soqotra Heritage Project)

3 Music plays an important part in the lives of the Socotri people (Soqotra Heritage Project)

4 Incense for sale, Hadiboh (Simon Urwin)

5 Dragon's blood powder mixed with milk is traditionally taken to stop bleeding after childbirth (Simon Urwin)

6 A traditional Socotri handshake: men clasp right hands and press foreheads and noses together (Nicole Smoot)

7   A packed stadium for the grand final of Socotra's football league (Chris Miller)

8 & 9   A girls' class and a carefully written exercise book at a Bedouin school (8 Hilary Bradt, 9 Nicole Smoot)

10   Socotri woman spinning locally sheared sheep's wool. Strips are then woven on a horizontal ground loom and assembled to make a carpet, rug or blanket (Soqotra Heritage Project)

1 Pots being crafted by hand (Chris Miller)

2 Bedouin camp at Firmihin Forest (Simon Urwin)

With thanks to Miranda Morris

LULLABY FROM A GRANNY VISITING HER FAMILY
A good day it was when we saw her face once more! Wherever she goes may her goats be of the most lucky and blessed kind!
Wherever she goes may there be bubbling water! May springs and pools of water rise up from the ground before her!
For her eyes are (as beautiful as) huge rain clouds clustering around the peaks of the high Haggeher in the morning.

itself. The more strict Islamic norms mean that it is no longer seen as acceptable for men and women to gather together, as before, to challenge one another in evening-long competitive poetry festivals. And the traditional occasions for the major poetry events – principally circumcision and wedding ceremonies – are no longer as they used to be: circumcision is now largely a private family affair, and at weddings it is more common to sing the types of (Arabic) song prevalent on the mainland.

As a result of modern education, and especially religious education, some islanders now feel ambiguous about their language; they welcome the spread of Arabic on the island and the new poetic forms from the mainland as a symbol of their having now joined the wider Muslim and Arabic-speaking communities of the Middle East. The poetry in the recently sponsored 'poetry competitions' in the capital, Hadiboh, has either been entirely in Arabic or else included poems in Arabic as well as those in a rather Arabic-influenced Socotri.

But it was through this language that island elders taught generation after generation of children how to maintain the necessary equilibrium between humans and the environment on this island in the middle of the sea. It was in Socotri that the fast-disappearing cultural traditions and socio-economic practices of the people of these islands were transmitted. This once self-sufficient community lived close to the natural environment for centuries. Of necessity they had to rely directly on it, not only for their survival, but also for their cultural and spiritual needs.

The continued survival of the Socotri language depends on its ability to hold its own against the Arabic that dominates its society, and to do so with, as yet, little official support or recognition. But it also depends on developing a script so that it becomes a written language, for it is certain that if speakers do not start to write in their own language, they will lose it altogether.

MUSIC AND DANCE *Julian Jansen van Rensburg and the Soqotra Heritage Project Team (page 46)*
Socotra is well known for its unique and rich poetry, but less so for its rich songs (A'adin/uh) and dancing (Reguze/uh) which can be performed by both men and women. These normally take place at wedding ceremonies, where women and men perform separately. The A'adin is often sung by two groups of men, who will repeat a verse to each other; this is normally accompanied by a jumping dance where two men, one from each side, will jump up and down in unison. The fishermen also have a traditional dance that can be traced to the mainland, involving two lines of men facing each other; they carry short sticks and, as they sing to each other while two or three drummers play, they approach and fall back. In the interior of the island is a traditional flute player, who is famed throughout Socotra and plays at weddings and festivals, while an old man who lives in Suq (Shiq in Socotri) is the best drum player on the island. The drum music and accompanying songs played in Suq (an

Dr Kay Van Damme

Friends of Soqotra (or Socotra, both spellings are used) or FoS is a non-profit UK-registered charity run entirely by volunteers, with members originating from Europe, the Middle East, Africa, Australia and the United States. It was established (in 2000) to promote the sustainable development and conservation of the Socotra archipelago's natural environment, and to support the environmentally friendly development of its inhabitants' lives. FoS also aims to bring together scientists studying Socotra and people with a more general interest, to exchange experiences and share their passion for the archipelago. It actively promotes co-operation with other international organisations that have the same aim, as well as local Socotri NGOs. The first AGM took place in 2001 and subsequently in different places internationally, often in scientific institutes: they are the world's only annual Socotra conferences. In 2018, the meeting was held for the first time in the Arab Region, at the Arab Centre for World Heritage in the Kingdom of Bahrain, with around 80 people of whom 13 were Socotri. The following year, in Palermo, Sicily, saw the launch of a global joint UNESCO-FoS awareness initiative, the **Connect2Socotra** campaign to highlight the importance of Socotra's unique biodiversity and culture. The meetings are always well attended by visitors from Yemen. Research, conservation and sustainable development of the island are among subjects discussed; anyone interested in Socotra and its natural and cultural heritage is welcome to attend, to contribute ideas and suggestions and to join the open discussions. See w friendsofsoqotra.org/Activities/Tayf_newsletter.html for past copies of the FoS newsletter *Tayf*, the Socotri word for aloe, which covers projects and activities on the island along with updates on scientific research.

Over the past 24 years, FoS has engaged in many small activities promoting the uniqueness of the archipelago's natural and cultural heritage as well as assisting its people. These have included projects to combat soil erosion, help in plant nurseries, produce information leaflets on nature and culture, deliver stethoscopes to the local hospital and sewing machines to the women's groups, support the folklore museum in Riqeleh, set up a boat repair workshop on Samha island to mitigate cyclone damage, and assist replantation schemes such as the mangrove site in Ghubbah. In addition, FoS committee members carry out independent research, producing scientific papers and information relevant to Socotra's conservation and biodiversity.

The annual budget is generally below US$6,000, funded by membership fees and small donations; FoS's most valuable resource is the combined passion and time given voluntarily by its members. Its website (w friendsofsoqotra.org) is extensive and, among the history, natural history, maps, background, links, information leaflets, activities etc, it includes extremely full and helpful guidelines for prospective visitors to the islands.

important centre of Socotri music and dance) are believed to have originated in Africa and are normally performed during weddings and other festivities.

LIFE ON SOCOTRA Because of its isolated location and seasonal harsh weather, in material terms Socotra has moved more slowly into the 20th and 21st centuries than much of the Arab mainland. Supplies must be brought in by air or sea and risk disruption during the stormy months; electricity can be erratic and Wi-Fi is sparse. Life can be hard. But the population is tight-knit and resourceful, finding ways through and around the obstacles. In rural areas fishing and animal husbandry are still essential sources of livelihood and components of the island's economy. Villagers belong to more than a hundred 'tribes', further divided into clans, with respected local leaders; communal decision-making is encouraged and meetings are held regularly to discuss local affairs.

There is more contact nowadays than previously between the rural inhabitants and the 'city dwellers' of Hadiboh, where the modern world has a stronger foothold. Ownership of modern cars, smartphones, televisions, labour-saving kitchen appliances and so forth is still relatively recent but increasing fast, in some cases through wives pressuring their husbands for a more comfortable life. Many of the traditional occupations described below are – sadly but inevitably – disappearing with the older generations who practised them, but the Soqotra Heritage Project team (page 46) is working to ensure that as many as possible are kept alive and drawn into the growing tourism sector. Livestock rearing remains linked to the pattern of the seasons, but with selected adaptations to the present day. Less traditional occupations with an eye on the future are found, among others, in government institutions, banks, small businesses, electronics, healthcare, transport, trade, education, construction of many kinds and tourism.

Traditional occupations *Miranda Morris*

Fishing In earlier times fishing was, with livestock rearing, one of the most important economic activities supporting the people of Socotra; the majority of northern coastal dwellers were full-time fishermen and many other islanders fished seasonally. People also dived in many of the lagoons, bays and sheltered reefs for oysters: the mother-of-pearl shell and pearls were sold to visiting trade boats. Today's fishing is on a larger scale. The artisanal fisheries target four principal resources: shark – primarily requiem sharks – kingfish, rock lobster and demersal reef fishes. These are sold for local consumption or to visiting boats which transport them to overseas markets. The earlier important trade in salted and dried fish and shark has declined, and the demand today is for fresh fish. During the summer southwest monsoon (May to September), the wild seas bring most offshore fishing to an end, and the shallow reef fishes migrate inshore to shallower waters where they are caught with fish-traps.

Livestock The principal livestock of the island was (as it still is) goats; cattle were herded in the central and eastern mountains and sheep along the coast and in the

MILK

For the Socotri people, milk (from cows and goats) has over the centuries been the most cherished and versatile item of their diet. Excluding **fresh milk** (not generally drunk as such) and **butter oil** (which was more generally used for trade or exchange than for consumption), its provision was sevenfold. First came **buttermilk**, the first stage of conversion from fresh milk and the basis for the remaining six, which consisted of boiled buttermilk, whey, soured buttermilk, **butter**, separated buttermilk, the **curd** from the separated buttermilk, and a dried **cheese** made from the curd. A similar 'nothing wasted' technique was applied to the source of the milk, with every possible part of the animal either eaten or put to some practical use.

drier eastern and western highlands. Donkeys and camels were reared as baggage animals, though some camels were also raised for milk in areas of the northern and southern coasts. Herders were frequently on the move with their animals in search of grazing and water and, in the long dry season when the pastures were grazed bare, spent much time gathering foliage and dried herbage to feed their animals. Breeding was carefully managed to ensure that livestock gave birth at the beginning of the winter rainy season. Livestock was reared principally for milk,

THE SOQOTRA HERITAGE PROJECT

Julian Jansen van Rensburg and the Soqotra Heritage Project Team

Socotra has been described as 'the forgotten island', a name equally relevant to its rich and unique cultural heritage, as well as the 'Galapagos of the Indian Ocean', an example of the focus often placed on the archipelago's natural (rather than cultural) heritage. Despite substantial interest over the past decade in recording and mapping the cultural heritage of Yemen, there has been only sporadic interest in that of Socotra – which is being severely impacted by the current conflict in mainland Yemen, the increasing demands for development on Socotra, and other external social and political influences. In recognition of this, the Soqotra Heritage Project (SHP), funded in 2017–2024 by the British Council's Cultural Protection Fund and led by the Royal Botanic Garden Edinburgh, began the huge task of documenting Socotra's rich tangible and intangible cultural heritage.

The first step was to equip a team of Socotri women and men with the skills necessary to assess and document the threats to their cultural heritage. These skills included conventional archaeological and ethnographic survey techniques, Kite Aerial Photography, 3D photogrammetry, and film production. Thus prepared, the SHP team have spent three years documenting over 400 hitherto unrecorded cultural heritage sites throughout Socotra. They have also been documenting Socotra's rich intangible traditions, which include carpet making, ceramics, salt production, aloe and dragon-blood resin harvesting as well as traditional games, never previously recorded. Any accompanying songs, stories and dialectical differences in the Socotri language were included. Much of the recording was done on film, used to promote awareness of these traditions. Many are in danger of dying out, for example those practised by elderly women whose children are leaving the countryside in search of better opportunities in Hadiboh or even in the Gulf.

All of this information has been stored in a dedicated database, an important resource that will help Yemen's General Organisation of Antiquities and Museums (GOAM) and local government officials to better manage their cultural heritage. It also highlights the areas and traditions which, despite the huge amount of work already done, are still undocumented and/or unrecorded, in part because Socotri is not a written language.

The SHP team can claim a number of firsts for Socotra, for example the women who have helped produce films about Socotra's heritage are the first Socotri filmmakers in the world. The team also initiated the creation of the first cultural heritage protected area, Deda'ahneten, one of the largest rock art sites on Socotra (page 86). It was on the verge of being destroyed by development, so the SHP team brought together local landowners, GOAM and officials from the Socotra Governorate to establish a protected area. The site is also used to promote awareness in schools, several of which have already visited. In addition, at this and

from which the owners extracted the butter oil which they traded for cereals and other necessities. This meant that most male young, of all species, were slaughtered soon after birth, so at this time of year the islanders had plenty of meat and milk.

Dates Wherever there was adequate water and soil, the old-time fishery and livestock were supplemented by date-palm and finger-millet cultivation. In the past, apart from the honey robbed from wild bee nests, or wild fruits and the nectar

other potential tourist sites, visitors will find interpretation boards designed and set up by the SHP team.

The SHP has also helped with the continuation of Socotra's annual cultural heritage festivals, which showcase not only Socotri poetry and language but also traditional dancing, music and singing. In addition, theatre workshops for local children have allowed younger and older generations to re-connect through shared traditional storytelling, thus spreading Socotri songs and stories throughout local communities. The success of this was measured in tears, as many of the older generation had thought that their songs and stories would die with them; they were overjoyed to share them with the younger generation, who had always been 'too busy with their phones' to learn about their past and traditions.

With increasing numbers of tourists visiting Socotra, the SHP team has been working with local communities, tour guides and governmental officials to promote sustainable and profitable cultural tourism, making Socotra's unique cultural heritage also a driver of sustainable development. With the same objective, inputs from the SHP team also play an important role in this guidebook.

We, the Soqotra Heritage Project team, have accomplished a great deal but there is always more to be done. The more we learn about Socotra's past, the more we remain focused on the future, and on ensuring that Socotra's tangible and intangible cultural heritage can be enjoyed by all generations from all corners of the world. Please help us by learning about our culture, supporting our local craftspeople, and respecting our historic sites by taking only photos and leaving only footprints.

THE SHP LADIES
Ahdab Salem Saeed Awadh Al-Ameri Qalansiyah Women's Institute
Shaikhah Mubarak Omar Sulaiman Hadiboh Women's Institute

THE SHP GENTLEMEN
Ahmed Eissa Ahmed Saeed Al-Rumaili
Ahmed Saeed Ahmed Al-Orqbi GOAM
Ali Mohammed Salem Hasan
Mohammed Talee Hasan Ali
Ismael Mohammed Ahmed Salem
Dr Julian Jansen van Rensburg Chronicle Heritage

Learn more about the project here: w socotraculturalheritage.org
Meet the team: w youtube.com/watch?v=XYFJtRnvSZQ
Learn about local handicrafts: w youtube.com/watch?v=PJGQNcj7vzg

sucked from flowers, dates were the only source of sweetness on the island. Men climbed the tall date-palms to fertilise the flowers and to harvest the fruit, supporting themselves on slings made from plaited cow hide. There were communally owned date-palm plantations as well as private ones, and there were penalties for allowing livestock to get into them. All the palms of any one area were harvested at the same time, so the many islanders who owned no date-palms could travel from area to area gleaning fallen dates and working at the harvest in exchange for a share of the produce. In earlier years terraces were built for the cultivation of finger-millet, and tobacco was also grown. In the larger villages and towns, some islanders planted small gardens and grew sweet potatoes, onions, all sorts of cucurbits and climbing beans, as well as bushes of basil to perfume the home.

Plant products In addition to dried and salted fish and butter oil, the islanders also used to trade aloe sap, frankincense gum and the resin of Dracaena ('dragon's blood') trees. Tamarind pods, wild oranges and the fruit of the spiny Christ's thorn plant as well as certain edible roots and tubers were gathered for sale in local markets. Islanders made charcoal, quicklime and lime mortar, and they gathered and prepared timber, using the many hard woods of the island to fashion wooden tools and shape the highly valued herding sticks. Women collected firewood for home use and sale, and plaited date-palm fibre into all kinds of mats and baskets. They made fine mats from the hides of their animals, tanned and stitched skins into a variety of bags and satchels, and plaited fine leather threads to make highly prized belts. They worked local clay by hand into pots of all sizes, and spun sheep wool to weave rugs for their own households and for sale. Specialists prepared medicinal and cosmetic mixtures from leaves, roots and fruits, and men worked goat horn to make handles for their precious knives. Salt was harvested from the sea, and medicinal rock salt from caves.

Wildlife The civet was trapped and milked of the thick secretion from its anal pouch: this with its strong musky smell was in great demand overseas for perfumery and was bought by trading boats for sale in East Africa, Aden and the Gulf. Cunning traps and snares were set for many different sorts of sea and land birds. At the right time of year men scaled the sheer sea cliffs in the dark to catch the plump shearwater nestlings that crouched on narrow ledges. At times of hunger, freshwater crabs and land snails were collected and eaten to stave off starvation.

Relaxation Life was often hard, but the winter rains and the birth of young livestock heralded a time of plenty and relaxation. Weddings were arranged, and celebrations were held, with night-long singing and dancing. The islanders competed against each other in racing and leaping contests, but also in poetry. Poetry and song were part of everyday life on the island, a natural way of communicating with others, be they human, animal, spirits of the dead, *jinn*, sorcerers or the divine.

Many of these traditional occupations have now disappeared or changed. However, one aspect of the island way of life remains unaltered: the islanders are still known for the warm welcome they give visitors.

Traditional sport and games *Julian Jansen van Rensburg and the Soqotra Heritage Project Team*

Games are considered one of the bridges through which customs and traditions are passed from one generation to another. The traditional games on Socotra constitute an important element of Socotri heritage and society. With the beginning of modernity and civic life in Socotra in the last quarter of the last century, folk games were at risk of being forgotten. Through recent work by the Soqotra Heritage Project the traditional games have been not only recorded but also reinvigorated and you can find them being played throughout the island, although football is still the most popular sport and there are several local teams on the island. Some of these games involve manual dexterity, using sticks and stones, and others are often played competitively between villages. Three of them are ones that energetic visitors could join:

Manfiga This game highlights a person's ability to jump. It is named after the rocks (Manfiga), which are connected to folk tales of people jumping on them in the past. To play this a group of young men choose a rock between 1 and 1.5m high. A player starts running towards it from an unspecified distance away, keeping his feet parallel to the ground before the jump and as he lands on the rock.

Magmiha This game is a battle between two players, each trying to bring his opponent to the ground by wrapping his arms around the opponent's waist, turning him around or lifting him and then bringing him to the ground.

Algashal This game has a few variants, but the basis is the same. Several (up to six) small stones are chosen. All but one are put on the ground and one is held in the player's hand. The stone in the hand is then tossed up and the player grabs either all or one of the rocks on the ground before catching the thrown stone. The person who is able to grab the most stones either in one go or over the course of several throws is considered the winner.

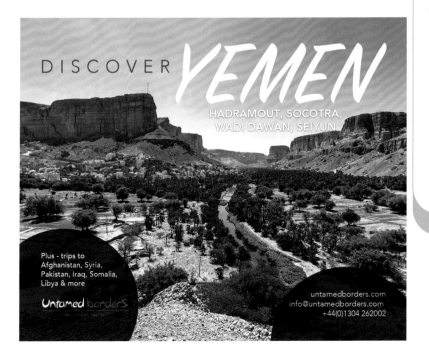

DISCOVER *YEMEN*

HADRAMOUT, SOCOTRA, WADI DAWAN, SEIYUN

Plus - trips to Afghanistan, Syria, Pakistan, Iraq, Somalia, Libya & more

Untamed borders

untamedborders.com
info@untamedborders.com
+44(0)1304 262002

1

2

Practical Information

Sweet it is when the pastures are safe and free from fear.
Sweet and peaceful then is sleep,
For the one who lets his goats out of a fine red fold while he plays on a pipe.

An old Socotri poem (translation by Miranda Morris)

WHEN TO VISIT

The climate dictates your holiday plans! **Late January to mid-May** are the best months, with wildflowers at their most colourful in January/February (although the desert rose flowers in February and March). From June to September there are very fierce monsoon winds, strong enough to disrupt transport and damage property, and uncomfortably high temperatures. Some of Socotra's residents leave the island during these months and while no international tour operators run trips during this off-season, it is possible to find local operators who are willing to. Note that if you do visit during this time of year, you will likely need to base yourself in a hotel or one of the eco-lodges, as the wind will make camping impossible. October and November will see some heavy rain, but not constantly; it fills the wadis and sharpens the colours, landscapes are lush and hiking in the mountains is good. December is the wettest month, with probable extensive flooding. However – this is weather, and nothing is guaranteed! There may be bursts of unseasonable rain or wind at any time, or (generally in October–December) cyclones.

HIGHLIGHTS

The following are the authors' favourite places, but there's pleasure in the smaller unexpected things too (the desert roses are a consistent delight) so remember to pause sometimes and just look at what's around you.

ARHER SAND DUNES *(Page 109)*
Towering sugar-white dunes have somehow travelled across the road and stacked themselves against the side of a mountain. Brave souls climb up for the slide down; others admire their efforts from the campsite below.

DETWAH LAGOON *(Page 138)*
A marine wonderworld of strange marine creatures: puffer fish, squid, sea cucumbers, swimming cowries and lots of stingrays. Plus Ellai the Caveman to show you the area and introduce you to his ocean-dwelling friends.

FIRMIHIN AND DAKAM FORESTS *(Pages 116 and 132)*
Both are home to stunning dragon's blood trees set against rocky canyons and the Haggeher Mountains. Firmihin Forest is easily accessible and commonly included in itineraries, while Dakam Forest, though harder to reach, rewards those willing to hike there with its peacefulness and breathtaking scenery.

HAGGEHER MOUNTAINS *(Page 3)*
Rising to over 1,500m high, these craggy peaks form the backdrop of many iconic Socotri scenes, even if you don't have time to join a camel trek to pass through them at close quarters.

HOMHIL PLATEAU (NATURE SANCTUARY) *(Page 94)*
The place that has it all: dragon's blood trees, chubby bottle trees clinging to salmon-pink rocks, and the extraordinary 'infinity pool' for swimming.

HOQ CAVE *(Page 108)*
Socotra has been described as 'like a Swiss cheese' because of all the holes and caves in its limestone. Hoq is a wonderful amalgamation of the standard cave delights of stalagmites and stalactites, with a rich history of early habitation to spike the imagination.

QALANSIYAH *(Page 137)*
You don't go to Socotra for its towns – or certainly not Hadiboh – but Qalansiyah, at its western tip, is an agreeably laid-back fishing village of stone-built houses, colourful doors and friendly people.

ZAHEQ OR STEROH *(Pages 134 and 135)*
Desert-like sand dunes: unlike the huge dunes at Arher, Zaheq and Steroh's dunes are smaller and easy to climb. There are so many though that you might wonder if you've somehow ended up in a pale version of the Sahara. They're especially beautiful during sunrise and sunset.

RAS ERISSEL *(Page 111)*
At the extreme eastern tip of the island two oceans meet: the Arabian Sea and the Indian Ocean. This rocky peninsula is beaded with sandy beaches, often covered with fragments of coral and shells, with dramatic breakers as a backdrop.

DIHAMRI MARINE NATURE SANCTUARY *(Page 107)*
Socotra's coral reef may be small, but it is undisturbed and, on the rare calm days, offers terrific snorkelling. The beach gives a preview of the reef, being entirely covered by fragments of coral, shells, and other colourful remains of marine life.

SHU'AB BEACH *(Page 151)*
Surely one of the most beautiful beaches in the world. The boat trip from Qalansiyah is part of the treat: brown boobies and Socotran cormorants pose on the pink cliffs and spinner dolphins accompany the boat. The sandy beach is sprinkled with shells and coloured pebbles. Perfect for a swim.

WADI KILLISAN *(Page 97)*
Don't miss the chance to visit the deep pools that collect in Socotra's Wadi Killisan, its easily the best fresh water swimming you'll find on the island. It takes a bit of effort to get there, but is hugely rewarding.

TOUR OPERATORS

There has been a big surge recently in companies that offer tours to Socotra, so the following lists are by no means complete. All the international operators noted here have been running Socotra trips for some years now, and the local operators listed have tourism licenses and are able to apply for your visas directly themselves. They can all help with your flights between the mainland and Socotra, and most international ones can deal with other international flights too if necessary (we found it more flexible to get our own).

INTERNATIONAL

Culture Road w cultureroad.nl
Inertia Network w inertianetwork.com. Very informative website.
Lupine Travel w lupinetravel.co.uk
Native Eye w nativeeyetravel.com

Pioneer Expeditions w pioneerexpeditions.com
Untamed Borders w untamedborders.com
Welcome to Socotra w welcometosocotra.com
Z Adventures w z-adventures.org. Organises 'Socotra Challenge' trips for the Socotra Marathon.

THE HISTORY OF TOURISM IN SOCOTRA   *Benjamin Carey (page vi)*

Socotra has always been an easy sell as a tourism destination. It is spectacularly beautiful, genuinely unique and remarkably difficult to reach.

The archipelago is a world away from the Yemeni mainland both physically and temperamentally. When, in the early 2000s, the Government of Yemen started to consider tourism as a possible driver of economic development, the then tourism minister's instinct was to prohibit it on Socotra. Yemen even seriously considered forgoing tourism in order to protect Socotra's extraordinary natural heritage. However, Socotra being so extremely marketable, flight schedules expanded and even cruise ships started to call. When UNESCO inscribed the Socotra Archipelago as Yemen's fourth World Heritage Site in 2008, tourism to Socotra really started to take off.

A host of international agencies arrived to write tourism strategies that mostly ignored the island's equally significant cultural heritage, while largely failing to build any local tourism-management capacity. As well as some more serious birding itineraries, a few specialist products emerged, including fishing, paragliding and diving. However, with limited rescue services, let alone a decompression chamber, and very limited medical facilities, many of these had minimal potential.

For a while, cruise ships began to call, but the rise of Somali piracy made insurance too expensive and the market quickly sailed away. Insurance has always been a challenge, not because of actual danger on Socotra but because foreign governments are bad at geography. An incident 500km away on the mainland would cause travel advisories to proscribe travel to the entire country including Socotra. The real risks for visitors are invariably natural, with flooding and cyclones often leading to flight cancellations.

The 2011 film *Salmon Fishing in the Yemen* again put the country in the spotlight, and the Ministry of Tourism took the opportunity to promote Socotra as an adventure tourism destination. This resulted in many enquiries about the quality of salmon fishing in Yemen and lots more visitors to Socotra.

The Soqotra Heritage Project (page 46) has reminded us that the cultural heritage of Socotra's people is arguably more important than the extraordinary landscapes and the more famous natural heritage, and is what makes Socotra such an extraordinary place to visit. Yemen is keen to share its heritage with the world; in return, the world has a responsibility to treat Socotra and its people with respect and sensitivity.

Practical Information   TOUR OPERATORS

2

SCHEDULED TOURS These tend to last either one or two weeks and have pre-planned itineraries, shown in detail on the operators' websites together with prices. The timing is often tight because there is a lot to fit in. The **one-week** scheduled tours cover the main sites: Hadiboh and Ayhaft canyon (*Chapter 3*); Qaria lagoon, Homhil, Hoq Cave, the eastern tip and Dihamri or Rosh marine nature sanctuaries (*Chapter 4*); the mountainous central area, Diksam Plateau and the southern coast (*Chapter 5*); and Qalansiyah, Detwah lagoon and the boat trip to Shu'ab beach (*Chapter 6*). Beyond this different operators may cater for different interests (whether hiking, camel trekking, swimming, snorkelling, plants, insects, marine life, fishing, local people etc); check their websites, or ask. For a camel trek in the interior you need to do a **two-week** scheduled tour (when the timing is more leisurely), skip some other visits or opt for a tailor-made tour. It currently isn't possible to visit the outer islands (page 152), but if they reopen to visitors then allow several extra days to travel by boat to see them. You will likely need to arrange everything in advance; check with your tour operator on the current situation.

ACTIVITIES AND TAILOR-MADE TOURS A tour tailor-made for you by your operator (for example if you travel with family or friends, so that you can agree beforehand what you want to see or do) can raise the cost, especially if booked with an international operator, but is far more flexible. Your first choice then is between camping at various sites around the island or staying in one of the hotels or eco-lodges on the north coast and driving to the sites each day; see page 66 for more about this.

For the energetic, there are walks, treks (including multi-day treks with camels into the mountains), swimming and snorkelling (weather-dependent) and scuba diving. If you're prepared to bring your own equipment, surfing, kite-surfing and paragliding are also possible. Information on these latter activities is limited, but we heard from some locals that the surf is not very consistent and some locations can be challenging, so do your research beforehand. Kite-surfing is likely to be more successful as there's almost always good wind to be found somewhere on the island – perhaps even too much at times. There are some excellent paragliding options such as from Momi Plateau, Ras Erissel and Wadi Dirhur (see w youtube.com/watch?v=MNjoXlVocGg).

Perhaps somewhat surprisingly, there's also the possibility of taking a gyrocopter flight, after a few were brought over by the UAE. From their open-air cabins you can get spectacular aerial views of the Haggeher Mountains, or even spot whale sharks out at sea. The price at the time of writing was around US$150 for a 30-minute flight – check with your tour operator for the latest details and bookings. The same

With its rich marine life and extensive coral reefs, Socotra offers some exceptional diving opportunities. The main base for diving is at Dihamri, where there is a dive centre with equipment for hire that was originally brought to the island for marine surveying use by the Socotra Conservation and Development Programme (SCDP). This equipment can be used at any of the dive sites in Socotra. There are two qualified dive masters on the island, Fouad and Naseem, and while it can be possible to organise going diving once you arrive, we strongly recommend you book in advance through your tour operator. Costs per dive are around US$100–170 (March 2024) depending on whether from shore or boat, including your equipment hire.

March to May are generally considered the best months for diving, when the water is usually calm and clear. Some of the best dive locations are:

Dihamri Marine Nature Sanctuary (page 107), which has two locations that can be dived straight from the shore at around 5–15m deep, and about another ten accessed by boat that vary from 15–40m. About 80% of the archipelago's coral reefs are here, and you have good chances of seeing a huge variety of fish, sponges, rays, blacktip, whitetip and nurse sharks, and turtles. Diving at Dihamri can be combined with additional dives on the same day at the nearby Rosh.

Rosh Marine Nature Sanctuary (page 107) has a 2km-long reef that runs parallel to the coast, about 1km offshore, so a boat trip is required. Despite the distance offshore, the depths are generally only around 10–15m, though can reach up to 40m in some places. There are some very large corals, along with many fish species, sharks, rays and other marine life to be seen.

Shu'ab beach (page 151) has only one dive site, about 2km from the shore, but it has Socotra's biggest shipwreck, the "Sunrise", about 150m long by 50m wide. A large number of fish can be seen on this artificial reef including large groupers, guitarfish and huge skates.

Ras Erissel (page 111) has seven dive locations. Due to the shallow and historically uncharted waters, there are a huge number of shipwrecks to explore here, including some that are possible to enter.

In addition to the above, Adho has a couple of sites on offer, both about 30m deep, plus the outer islands Samha and Darsa (page 154) have good dive sites too, with vertical walls where large shoals of mantas can sometimes be seen. Wherever you choose to dive, it's worth bearing in mind that some of the dive sites can be deep or have strong currents, so check first and make sure you have the right level of experience for the sites you plan on diving.

Practical Information TOUR OPERATORS

2

company operating the gyros has an MI-2 helicopter available for hire; ask for availability and prices.

The island is a photographer's nirvana, everywhere you go, including at night, with exceptionally dark skies offering perfect conditions for astrophotography. Otherwise discuss your particular interests (botany, wildlife, archaeology, local

1   The campsite at Detwah lagoon, showing the large 'nest' tents (page 138) (Nicole Smoot)

2 & 3   Fresh fish and goat both feature heavily on the menu while you're camping, along with vegetables and salads (page 66) (2 Chris Miller, 3 Hilary Bradt)

4   Alfresco dining, Socotra style (Hilary Bradt)

1 Preparing for a boat trip to Shu'ab (page 151) (Chris Miller)

2 Trekking to the 'infinity pool' at Homhil (page 94) (Hilary Bradt)

3 A camel being unloaded after a trek (Chris Miller)

Wild camping, beneath a dragon's blood tree at Diksam Plateau (page 116) (Simon Urwin)

1 A gyrocopter flight offers a bird's eye view of the island (Chris Miller)

2 A beach clean-up is a great way to help the island (Hilary Bradt)

3 Tempting though it may be, the shells and coral washed up on Socotra's beaches are for photographs only. It is strictly forbidden to try to take them home (Chris Miller)

4 Locally made pottery makes an excellent souvenir (Chris Miller)

people, sea fishing, birds…) with your tour operator beforehand to see what can be arranged. We give you ideas throughout this book, and the websites of many of the tour operators and Friends of Soqotra (page 44) are also helpful.

RED TAPE: VISAS AND TRAVEL INSURANCE

You will need to obtain a **tourist visa** in advance of your trip. Only authorised Socotri tour operators can procure these, or an international operator who will be working with a local one on the ground anyway. The price will be included in the overall cost of your trip and, as the visas are currently only issued at most 30 days in advance, it will only be emailed to you a few weeks before your trip begins; make sure you print it and bring it with you. If you plan to go straight to a local operator, check with them that they are authorised to obtain visas – that status is renewed annually, so new ones may have joined or others dropped out by the time you read this. The same tour operator will also help you book your flights into Socotra from either Cairo or Abu Dhabi, as they are not available to book online. When booking with a local operator it is possible you will be put in contact with someone at the airline to pay them directly; in our case this involved making a transfer into a UAE bank account that they sent us over WhatsApp! Note that if travelling via Cairo, you are responsible for your **Egyptian visa**, which is currently very easy to obtain on arrival at Cairo airport and costs US$25 per entry.

For Yemen (including Socotra), at the time of writing you should not have any sign in your passport of having travelled to Israel, or you risk being refused entry. It's possible this may change in the future, as political allegiances alter; but meanwhile do check carefully. If the prohibition is still in force, it is likely to be applied stringently.

Insurance is tricky while both the UK and US governments are advising against travel to Yemen. Most insurers can't go against government advice. We used a US company, **Global Underwriters** (w globalunderwriters.com), which wouldn't insure citizens of the US but didn't object to those from the UK, although the premium was high for 'high-risk' Yemen. They also didn't have an upper age limit. In the UK, **Battleface** (w battleface.com) offer cover for UK citizens, as does **Voyager Insurance** (w highriskvoyager.com). You can also shop around among other insurers by searching for 'High Risk Travel Insurance' or 'Insurance against FCDO advice' online. Good medical insurance is strongly recommended, including emergency evacuation, because of Socotra's distance from the mainland, although some of our group went without it. However, the small hospital there is said to be good.

GETTING THERE AND AWAY

There are currently two airlines that fly to Socotra. **Air Arabia** (w airarabia.com) operate direct flights from Abu Dhabi to Socotra, generally twice a week (Tuesdays and Fridays) during the main tourist season, dropping to once a week (Tuesdays) during the off-season, though the frequency may have increased by the time you read this. Flight times vary somewhat but generally depart Abu Dhabi in the morning, and return to Abu Dhabi in the afternoon. **Yemenia Airways** (w yemenia.com) offer one flight a week to Socotra from Cairo via a stop at Aden in mainland Yemen to drop off/pick up passengers, and you'll likely be subject to some additional checks of your passport during the layover. In both cases the precise schedule of the flights is announced only a few months before departure. Your tour operator should advise you of the schedule once it becomes available, and we recommend booking as soon

2

after that as you can, as the flights do tend to fill up quite quickly. Arrival procedures at Socotra airport can be slow, especially if you're last off the plane, but are relatively hassle-free (page 75) and your guide should meet you in the carousel area.

There are no scheduled services to Socotra by **sea**, and trying to find a place on a **cargo boat** from the mainland is not recommended – it's unpredictable, slow, unreliable, extremely uncomfortable and possibly dangerous if piracy in the area flares up again.

Flights to and from Socotra can sometimes be delayed, or even cancelled, in either direction. This means that, going home, it is much safer to spend a night in Cairo or Abu Dhabi rather than to book your onward flight for the same day. Make sure you have some emergency cash in case you have to spend some extra time on Socotra due to a cancelled flight.

As of January 2024 there is a ban on the import and use of plastic bags. It didn't seem to be enforced while we were there, but be mindful of that if you are considering taking any with you. Also remember that you must not take any shells, stones or organic matter (plants, pufferfish…) away from Socotra; see page 163 for further details. Bags will be searched at the airport both when you arrive and as you leave. This can be slow, so get there in plenty of time when departing. (And bring a book in case the flight is then delayed.)

HEALTH

Socotra has fewer health hazards than the mainland of Yemen, but check with your GP or travel clinic which vaccines are currently recommended for the area: generally hepatitis A, hepatitis B, rabies and typhoid. Rabies vaccination before travel is highly recommended because post-exposure treatment is simpler and may be available locally if you are already vaccinated. As a seasoned traveller you are probably already up-to-date with routine vaccines such as tetanus, diphtheria, polio and MMR, but check with your doctor if in doubt. Polio has been detected in other parts of Yemen. If you have had confirmed dengue fever in the past, ask your travel clinic about dengue vaccination.

Malaria has been eliminated on Socotra but does still exist on the mainland, and hungry insects and ticks can still transmit other diseases. Day-biting mosquitoes may carry dengue virus and tiny sandflies can transmit leishmaniasis at night: seek medical advice if you develop a febrile illness or a non-healing skin lesion. Avoid insect bites by covering up with long sleeves and long trousers especially after sunset, using repellents (containing DEET or icaridin) on exposed skin and, if necessary, sleeping under a mosquito net.

Watch out for jellyfish when swimming, and take care on the sharp rocks when trekking. Check with your guide before bathing or paddling in fresh water, as this can put you at risk of a parasitic infection called schistosomiasis or Bilharzia. If you think you have been exposed, speak to your doctor or travel health clinic about testing: this should be done at least eight weeks after travel.

You should of course bring adequate supplies of any personal medication you may need, bearing in mind that if you miss your return flight it might be several days or more before there's space for you on another one. Health care on Socotra is best described as basic. There is a small modern hospital on the island – we even met a female dentist! You can find a few pharmacies and medical centres, and various charities bring in medical supplies from time to time, but don't expect extensive stocks. Check with your tour operator beforehand what kind of first-aid equipment they will have, and bring your own supplies anyway.

Drink bottled water or, much better, bring your own filter-topped bottle or purifying tablets. None of our group developed any stomach problems and we all ate whatever we were given. However it makes sense to take reasonable precautions with food: a good rule of thumb is 'peel it, boil it, cook it, or forget it'. Wash your hands or use hand sanitiser regularly. Most travellers' diarrhoea is self-limiting and only needs treatment with fluid and rehydration salts, eg: Dioralyte. Seek medical advice if diarrhoea is accompanied by fever, severe abdominal pain or blood in the stools, or if it persists beyond three days.

Avoid contact with animals. Rabies virus is transmitted through the saliva of mammals. Always wash the wound and seek medical help immediately if bitten, scratched or licked on broken skin by any mammal. Be guided by your tour operator and travel insurance. Post-exposure treatment includes a course of rabies vaccine. Supplies can be limited in Yemen, so you may need to leave the country for vaccination. Unvaccinated travellers may also need evacuation for additional treatment with rabies immunoglobulin (RIG). Remember, once you develop symptoms, rabies is always fatal.

TRAVEL CLINICS AND HEALTH INFORMATION A list of travel clinic websites worldwide is available on w istm.org. For other journey preparation information, consult w travelhealthpro.org.uk (UK) or w wwwnc.cdc.gov/travel (USA). All advice found online should be used in conjunction with expert advice received prior to or during travel.

SAFETY

The Yemeni (and particularly Socotri) tradition of courtesy to visitors makes this a particularly safe destination. Indeed, the first thing our guide said to us was: 'Socotra is the safest destination in the world! *In the world!*' There's no evidence of crime against tourists, and members of our group never felt in any way at risk. We (particularly women) can reciprocate the courtesy by conforming to local norms rather than imposing our own (see also page 65). In Hadiboh, women alone and with their heads and arms uncovered may be irritated by male scrutiny and comments – not unlike those encountered in rougher areas of England's cities some decades ago. The villages are gentler. In this strictly Muslim country overt displays of same-sex affection could cause offence and be potentially risky. If you've any concerns, have a word with your guide.

Even the usual risk of road traffic accidents is reduced here since there are very few cars on the road – and few roads where fast driving is possible. Your greatest danger is probably from falls on the sharp rocks – or, if like me, you are careless enough to trip over a tent's guy ropes during a hurried night visit! Do check with the locals before swimming in the ocean, as currents can sometimes be very strong.

One obvious bit of advice, but one that should be mentioned, is that on a politically unstable island it would be foolhardy to take photos at road checks or any military installations. Indeed, when your mobile phone bleeps 'Welcome to Saudi Arabia!' you can take it as a warning not to take a photo. If ever in any doubt, always ask your guide.

Travellers with disabilities will find few aids and adaptations but plenty of human help if they ask. The UK's **gov.uk** website (w gov.uk/government/publications/disabled-travellers/disability-and-travel-abroad) has a downloadable guide giving general advice and practical information for travellers with a disability (and their companions) preparing for overseas travel.

WHAT TO TAKE

When James Wellstead was preparing to travel round Socotra in 1834 he considered carefully.

> I studiously avoided bringing with me more than I absolutely required, *viz.* a few changes of linen, some provisions (in case we should find any scarcity on the island), my instruments for celestial and other observations, a small bed which answered also as a saddle (a mode which, by the way, I recommend to all travellers who have occasion to journey on camels), and a small tent which was considered indispensably necessary to shelter us at night from the dew.

You could possibly cut back on the heavy stuff. In fact, if you are considering going to Socotra you are probably a seasoned traveller anyway with your own routine for packing, so let us just remind you of a few suggested essentials.

PRACTICALITIES

- Day pack
- Waterproof bag for camera and electronics etc on boat trips
- A light sweater or fleece (it can be cold there, especially at higher altitudes and at night)
- A light, windproof and waterproof jacket
- Biodegradable wet wipes, toilet roll, hand sanitiser
- Sunscreen (preferably reef safe if you intend to swim or snorkel)
- Plug adapter (both continental 2-pin and UK 3-pin sockets exist)
- Water bottle with filter (to save on plastic bottles)
- Hiking poles (if you usually use them for walking)
- Head torch (night walks and Hoq Cave) plus hand-held torch and plenty of spare batteries
- At least three spare camera batteries plus powerbank/solar charger
- Towel (microfiber), mask and snorkel
- Shoes with thick soles or hiking boots for rough walks
- Sandals (not flip flops) or old trainers, for wading in lagoons
- **This guidebook** – and it would be kind to leave your copy on the island after your trip

FOR CAMPING Find out from your tour operator how hot/cold the campsites will be and whether they provide blankets. This determines whether you need to bring a warmer sleeping bag or just a sheet liner.

Also, since not all the campsites will have toilets...a note for the ladies (the chaps will just go and pee outside the tent). Many of us need to get up at night, but few relish the tramp around a dark campsite looking for a private spot. I (Hilary) solved the problem with a kitchen funnel and a bottle. And two matching screw tops, one that fitted the funnel stem and the other to keep the, um, effluent safe until it could be disposed of in the morning. I was smugly happy with this arrangement.

FOR CAMEL TREKKING Camel trekking includes tough hiking so, in addition to the usual trekking gear, Chris and Miranda recommend the following:

- Sturdy boots. Sometimes you will be grateful for waterproof ones and other times quick-draining boots are better. The choice is yours. Just make sure they have tough soles for the rough rock and stones.

- Warm and windproof clothing (this applies to any trip which goes into the highlands – which all treks do)
- Quick-drying hiking trousers (not jeans)
- Wind- and waterproof jacket and over-trousers
- Finally, protection against 'killer grass'. James Wellsted described it, in 1834: 'Around the upper part [of the stem] a number of radii branch forth, at the extremity of each of which is a sharp-pointed spire or prickle, also barbed. We found these a great pest and annoyance for they adhered with much tenacity to our clothes and frequently penetrated the flesh.' Finely woven synthetic trousers plus Gore-Tex shoes/boots gave us the best protection.

But remember, take as little as possible. It'll make life easier for the camels – and for you if you ever have to carry the gear.

COURTESY For women, we suggest bringing (for when you feel you should cover up) two long-sleeved, high-necked cotton tops, a head-scarf or head covering, and baggy (unrevealing) trousers/pants. General advice we've been given is that, for women, at least shoulders, arms, and legs to below the knee should be covered, in Hadiboh and villages. Shorts and low sleeveless tops should be saved for the beach. For men, short-sleeved shirts or T-shirts are fine, but shorts can be dodgy except on the beach.

MONEY AND BUDGETING

The currency is the **Yemeni rial**, whose rate against other currencies is fluctuating wildly just now (sometimes by 15% or so) because of the war on the mainland and inflation, so check it nearer the time of travel. The amount you can take into and out of Yemen is limited, and you can't buy rials beforehand in Cairo. Instead bring **US dollars**, which you can change into rials in Hadiboh. Just ask your guide to take you to a bank or exchange office. Make sure, however, that they are clean uncrumpled bills, 2009 series or newer, as older dated bills are not readily accepted. Any seemingly minor tears or pen marks on otherwise perfect looking notes can be problematic too, as the local money changer won't accept them; your tour operator may still take them but it is a bit awkward for them as they will then have to get them changed by someone over in the UAE. There are no ATMs or facilities for using credit/debit cards, and travellers' cheques are useless; it's important to stick to US$ cash. There's no facility for changing your rials back into dollars or Egyptian pounds when you are leaving (unless you can privately find someone who's going in the opposite direction), so you need to use them up on Socotra.

If you're unsure about how much cash to bring (and at present there's very little temptation to shop, except for a few souvenirs; pages 68, 69 and 83) then bring more US$ than you think you'll need, ask your guide's advice, change a small amount in Hadiboh to start with and then more if you need it, and take any leftover dollars home afterwards. Most necessities should be included in your tour package, but see *Shopping* (page 68). If you need an emergency (but not necessarily instant) top-up, both Western Union and MoneyGram are available in Hadiboh. For buying Egyptian currency if you need it, there are convenient facilities at Cairo airport.

Note that the payment process to tour operators can vary. The international ones tend to take a money transfer for some or all of your payment, while the local ones might need you to pay separately in advance for your flight and then bring US$ in cash for the tour fee, or perhaps transfer some or all of the total to an account in the UAE.

TIPPING You can use leftover rials as a tip or partial tip for your driver or guide when you leave (US$ are also fine for this). Otherwise (discuss this with your guide too), it's not part of the culture unless you want to reward some special service or person. Your tour operator will probably have a 'kitty' for tips (either US$ or rials) to be shared among the camping crew at the end; find out about this before you leave home, to make sure you'll have enough cash left over. If any of the crew have been particularly helpful, it's fine to give them a personal tip as well.

BARGAINING Ask your guide about this, but generally it's less aggressive than in many countries. You will be expected to bargain in the market for fruit or dates, but in Hadiboh's shops, prices are likely to be fixed, although in any more touristy ones you could ask for a reduction for quantity if you buy several items. In the Socotra Women's Association it isn't appropriate, except possibly for quantity, as the members are paid according to the items they have made. On the other hand, if someone comes up to you in the street with something dubious, be firm and offer what you feel is fair. Courtesy matters, always.

GETTING AROUND

Your tour operator will deal with this, using 4x4s that are suitable for the roads, some in better condition than others. There are some local mini-buses, departing from various stands in Hadiboh to serve local villages, but they mostly don't go to the tourist sites that you'll be visiting and drivers often speak no English. You may also spot school buses serving rural areas.

ACCOMMODATION

Socotra has seven small hotels and a few camps with small bungalows or caravans to stay in, all in or around Hadiboh on the north coast (page 77). More tourist hotels are likely to be constructed if disputes among developers and conservationists, local people and incomers can be settled, but – we suspect – not immediately. Meanwhile you are likely to be camping, which does save driving between your chosen attractions and Hadiboh every day – although some operators or individuals opt for this and, on a small island, it's perfectly possible. Some tour operators have large bell tents, or 'nests', which can comfortably take two or three people with space to stand up and move around. Others have smaller one-person or two-person tents. Some will provide full equipment (mattresses, pillows, blankets) and others much less. You need to check with them individually. In either case you will find a sheet sleeping bag useful. The campsites are mostly beautifully located, peaceful and with good views. Many of the campsites have basic facilities (bathroom, sun shelter and cooking area), but in others it's a case of 'back to nature'. We had persuaded our tour operator to bring a small 'toilet tent' (quite exciting in a strong wind…) and thoroughly recommend this.

EATING AND DRINKING

First and foremost, bear in mind that alcohol is not available for sale in Socotra, and, while it is now possible to bring some in via duty free, you should be discrete if you choose to do so as its consumption is generally frowned upon. Canned and bottled fruit drinks are available in all small shops, and your guide will provide water (or you can bring your own filter equipment). Some cafés/restaurants do good smoothies, in both Qalansiyah and Hadiboh, where if you're lucky, a cheery little ice-cream van may occasionally bustle by.

The climate and the ever-hungry goats mean that fruit or vegetables aren't grown in great quantities on Socotra (although there are some, including good tomatoes and watermelons), while a lot are imported from the mainland and therefore expensive. What the island does have in abundance is fresh fish and seafood (including tasty crayfish), as well as goat meat. Pasta and rice provide carbohydrate, embellished by tasty sauces or dips – and, of course, flatbread. Dates are plentiful; until relatively recently they and honey were the only sources of sweetness, as sugar was late in reaching the island.

The **Hadiboh restaurants** marked on the town map have fairly limited menus but are friendly and accommodating to foreigners, and both La Serina and the Summerland Hotel (page 77) do a practical buffet breakfast with bread, cheese, boiled eggs, dates, honey etc. The Summerland also serves dinner in its own restaurant. The other hotels use restaurants nearby. Otherwise you will be eating picnic meals prepared by your tour operator's camping team – and you won't go hungry, but there's a limit to what foods they can trundle round the countryside in 4x4s or get from local villagers so there's not a huge variety. However, on our trip they rustled up some good goat stew, fried chicken and various chunks of fish with pasta or rice, along with fresh salad. This was followed by traditional Socotri sweet tea or instant coffee, with sweetened condensed milk providing a childhood treat. If you're lucky enough to be there during the short (and varying) lobster season, you might end up especially well fed. It's becoming quite expensive though, and depending on which fishing village you are trying to buy from, you might also find that their entire quota has been reserved for sale to the Saudis or UAE.

TRADITIONAL FOOD

Julian Jansen van Rensburg and the Soqotra Heritage Project Team

In the interior of the island, the Socotri eat a variety of local plants, and when there is a wedding or a special guest arrives they will often slaughter a goat. The selection, slaughtering and cooking of the goat follow specific rules and customs that include the Islamic practice of cutting the throat to let the blood drain out. The whole goat carcass including the offal is used by the Socotri; nothing is wasted. Once cut into pieces the entire carcass is boiled. The juice is served first, followed by the bones, for which a rock can be provided to help guests to crack them open and remove the marrow. This is then followed by the meat and offal, which the host cuts and serves on a communal dish of rice; it may be accompanied by yoghurt and/or ghee. This is all eaten with the right hand, although Western guests may be given a spoon.

When a guest arrives in a home, the host welcomes him or her by offering very sweet tea, the sweeter the better. Milk in tea is normally offered only by the interior inhabitants, who drink a very sweet milky tea throughout the day. The milk is normally taken directly from the goats and heated up in a traditional Socotri pot, before being mixed with tea and sugar.

Vegetarians can be catered for but with very little variety, so could consider bringing snacks from home or buying them in Hadiboh. If you've any particular food requirements, do mention them to your tour operator beforehand so that any necessary preparations can be made.

SHOPPING

Socotra is unusual in that there are very few places, at present, to spend your rials. Until we were taken to the **Socotra Women's Association** (page 83), we found almost nothing we wanted. **Dates** are a good bet, although they may come from the mainland (but are still delicious, around US$3 a pack), and **honey** is the most prized local souvenir although very expensive – it can be up to US$30 a kilo, depending on quality, and is even bought by royalty in neighbouring mainland countries. If you plan to buy some (smaller quantities are available), it's good to have a screw-top plastic bottle to decant it into for taking home. The Honey Center in Hadiboh was started with help from the French Embassy in 2007, co-operates with local bee-keepers and has helpful details about the various grades of honey – it also sells some other souvenirs. **Foutas** (men's skirts) look good on women too and cost around US$40, while a full *abaya* and *niqab* for women costs around US$35, always depending on the currency exchange rate at the time. The small shops dotted around Hadiboh had a variety of attractive fabric items and accessories and some rather glitzy metalwork when we were there, but are likely to become more tourist-conscious. The Summerland Hotel was making an effort with a T-shirt and some faded postcards. However, you won't be able to buy stamps or send cards at present as the post office is closed because of the mainland war. If tourism picks up then surely an entrepreneur will get going with decent souvenirs.

For non-souvenir shopping, Hadiboh's all-purpose shops are relatively well stocked with basic necessities but staff don't necessarily speak any English.

MEDIA AND COMMUNICATIONS

Mobile coverage is available from Yemeni providers as well as Etisalat from the UAE – mostly in Hadiboh and around the larger towns – and is compatible with most (but currently not all) international providers. Already you will see young local people glued to their phones. At present no local SIM cards are available for visitors to buy, however you can pick up an Etisalat SIM while passing though Abu Dhabi, or an eSIM online before travelling. Don't expect too much from it though; for a lot of your trip you won't have any signal, and even when you do it'll likely prove frustratingly slow. **Wi-Fi** availability has improved in the last few years, with most hotels now having it in common areas, or if you are lucky even your room. We didn't find it especially reliable though, and you may have to pay a small fee. You also can't communicate with the outside world by 'snail mail'; the **post office** is closed because of the war on the Yemen mainland.

CHARGING FACILITIES There is electricity in Hadiboh, Qalansiyah and some larger villages (sockets are a mix of UK 3-pin and continental 2-pin), but for charging appliances and camera batteries, keen photographer Chris says: 'Apart from our first night in Summerland Hotel we didn't get a chance to do any mains charging for the whole two weeks. Instead we used a powerbank and solar charger which together provided more than enough power for our phones and camera batteries.' You can also use the charging socket in your vehicle while driving; bring an adaptor for this.

Julian Jansen van Rensburg and the Soqotra Heritage Project Team

On Socotra there is a rich tradition of handicrafts that are sometimes available to buy. We would recommend that you purchase these from the local Women's Institutions, where you will be directly supporting the ladies who are making them; see w soqotraculturalheritage.org/crafts and page 83.

CARPETS AND RUGS The Socotri rugs are part of an age-old tradition that was first recorded in the 10th century, when the Yemeni geographer, historian and astronomer al-Hamdānī (d 945) listed them among the island's major exports. Weaving on Socotra is traditionally done only by women; they use a horizontal ground loom, one of the earliest known weaving methods in the world, dated to around 4400BC. The whole process of weaving a rug takes several weeks, from washing and shearing the sheep, sorting the wool according to colour, carding it, spinning it, and finally weaving strips on the ground loom before fitting them together to make a rug. The texture of the wool will determine whether the rug is used as a floor mat, or as a blanket for those cold winter evenings in the mountains. Every time a rug is made the ladies sing a traditional Socotri song, thus giving each rug its own distinctive story. Currently the manufacturing of these rugs is under threat as few elderly ladies remain who are able to make them. The Soqotra Heritage Project has documented this process, which you can see on their website (page 46). A good place to buy woven products is in the village of Nissam, Ras Erissel (page 113).

POTTERY Traditional Socotri pottery has been made and used on Socotra for millennia, and archaeologists have found pottery similar to that in use today in some of the earliest ruins on the island. It is back-breaking work that is traditionally done only by women; they have to walk several hours just to find a suitable area to get clay and temper, and bring this back to the village to begin making the pottery. The type of temper added to the clay and the methods used in making the pots differ between each region on the island. Typically, the women either make pots for storage or heating and drinking milk and food, or incense burners. However, today you can also purchase model dragon's blood trees, Egyptian vultures and even camels. Pottery is normally decorated with designs made using shells before it is fired in a bonfire. It is then sometimes further decorated using either the juice of crushed plant leaves (often *Jatropha unicostata* and occasionally *Withania* species that are endemic to Socotra) or dragon's blood resin, which is applied directly to the pot as it comes out of the bonfire.

There is a good demonstration of pottery-making and other crafts on Socotra in this YouTube video: w youtube.com/watch?v=PJGQNcj7vzg, and you can visit the Delfadehin Pottery Association (page 83) where you can see it being made in person and also purchase items.

MEDIA If you're camping you won't have much opportunity to see it, but **television** does exist, at least in Hadiboh and Qalansiyah. In our room at the Summerland Hotel, we were able to pick up some news (and other) channels in English, although reception was poor. With only a few incoming flights a week, obviously there are no daily newspapers in any language.

CULTURAL ETIQUETTE

We wouldn't dream of telling you how to behave! But some human reactions vary from country to country, so here are a few of our hints for Socotra. It's a place still relatively new to tourism, so our visits can have repercussions for those of future tourists. There is also a helpful section for visitors on the Friends of Soqotra website w friendsofsoqotra.org.

CLOTHING Women tourists come back from Socotra saying 'I never covered my head and it was fine', or men say 'My girlfriend had bare arms and no-one bothered her.' Well, of course! The Socotri people are naturally courteous and don't want to embarrass guests. But I, Janice, remember the relief on my young driver's face and his spontaneous 'thank you' when I put on a head-scarf as we approached Hadiboh from the countryside, and Miranda, who wore one, was congratulated by the village women. Local women, particularly in Hadiboh, are almost all completely covered in *niqabs* and *abayas*, so our more visible flesh can be disconcerting. I felt more comfortable in Hadiboh covered up, with a wrap-around scarf, long-sleeved blouse and baggy trousers, but you may not. It's a personal choice and there are no rules. To my mind, courtesy to the Socotri people is the key.

CHILDREN AND GIFTS Probably everyone knows by now that you should not turn children into beggars or trigger jealousies by giving sweets, pens etc to individuals, however cute they may be. This is important on Socotra, where kids have not yet learnt to expect gifts and dental care is still limited. There are other ways of raising a smile, and it's much better to take school materials to a school so they can be properly shared. Even then, check with your tour operator that it's not always the same schools that get the visits and the gifts; there will be less tourist-friendly ones that are equally needy and where reactions are more spontaneous. Learn how to ask 'What is your name?' (page 162), which kids will enjoy telling you.

COURTESY The extremely polite Socotri people are tolerant of our sometimes different norms of behaviour. There are ways we can reciprocate. For example, rudeness and anger are considered bad form and will achieve nothing. And as in any country you visit, it's good to learn a few polite or friendly words in Socotri or Arabic. 'Hello' and 'thank you' are internationally important! Even without them, take time for a smile and an appreciative glance around before you make a direct request, for example in a shop.

Remember too that in this strictly Muslim country your guide and/or driver will most probably want to pray regularly during the day, wherever you are, so be understanding about this.

SHAKING HANDS Be careful. There are men who don't want to shake women's hands and vice versa. If in doubt, let whoever you are greeting take the lead.

TAKING PHOTOS Foreigners looming up with cameras or phones is becoming a more familiar sight and some people don't mind – some even request a photo – but others do object, sometimes strongly, so you should always ask beforehand and respect their decision. Particularly, don't photograph women unless you are quite sure they are happy with it. Officially it's not allowed, so if they (or anyone who is watching) look at all fearful or reluctant, apologise and move away.

THE GENDER GAP   As apparently liberated Western women we tread an awkward path, falling somewhere between Socotri men and Socotri women so that neither quite knows how to treat us, nor we them. Adjusting can take time. Men have it much easier! (Except that I remember the terror of heavily veiled teenage schoolgirls when the entirely unthreatening men in our group entered their classroom.) Every encounter is different, not all are easy, and probably the best advice is just to be yourself. Socotra is a beautiful country with lovely people. Go and see!

BEING USEFUL   Just by going to Socotra and buying local products and services, we are useful. If you can, please leave your copy of this guide behind on the island, whether with your guide or driver or with anyone else who wants it. When your visit is almost over, think what might be useful on the island and that you don't really need. For example Chris donated some unwanted first-aid equipment to a small local pharmacy at Ras Erissel. Torches, batteries, notebooks, snorkel and mask…? You can leave things with your tour operator to pass on. If you want to stay in touch with the island, you could consider joining Friends of Soqotra (page 44).

Traveling **Socotra**

Travel to Socotra with us
www.travelingsocotra.com

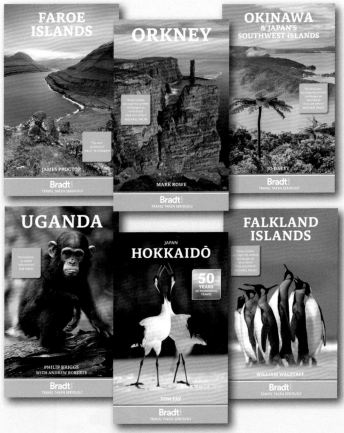

Part Two

THE GUIDE

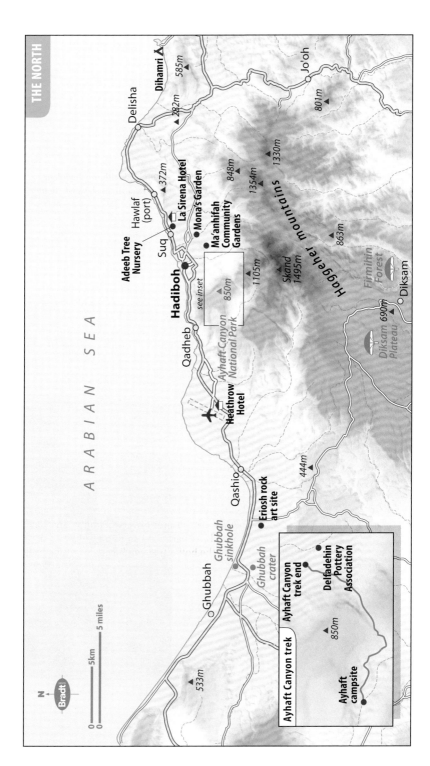

ARABIAN SEA

Dihamri ▲

585m ▲

Delisha

282m ▲

Jo'oh

801m ▲

372m ▲

Hawlaf (port)

La Sirena Hotel

Mona's Garden

848m ▲

1330m ▲

Adeeb Tree Nursery

Suq

Ma'anhifah Community Gardens

1354m ▲

Haggeher mountains

863m ▲

Hadiboh

see inset

850m ▲

1105m ▲

Skand 1495m ▲

Firmihin Forest

Diksam

Qadheb

Ayhaft Canyon National Park

Diksam 690m ▲

Diksam Plateau

Heathrow Hotel

Qashio

444m ▲

Ghubbah

Ghubbah sinkhole

Eriosh rock art site

Ghubbah crater

533m ▲

N

Bradt

0   5km
0   5 miles

Ayhaft Canyon trek

Ayhaft Canyon trek end

Delfadehin Pottery Association

850m ▲

Ayhaft campsite

3

The North

> I never witnessed a more magnificent sight than a walk of two hours [has] afforded me… It blew fresh this morning, and a heavy rolling sea tumbled with much violence on the rocks below us. The roar of the waters, though we were at times elevated about two hundred feet, was almost deafening; the white spray flew to the height of thirty or forty feet…
>
> Lieutenant James Wellsted, 1834 (walking from what is now Hadiboh to Qadheb)

This area contains what is very much the 'business zone' of Socotra, with the airport, the capital Hadiboh and the port relatively close together along a well-made coastal road, beside which more new buildings (including hotels) are being constructed. The various national flags in evidence (UAE, Saudi Arabia, South Yemen, Yemen and probably more by the time you read this) give you an idea of how coveted this small but valuable island is. Eventually the stretch between the airport and the port seems likely to be fully built up, at least on the inland side, so containing the development within a single area, but meanwhile there are still some good sea views and patches of characteristic Socotra countryside.

ARRIVAL

Fortunately for tired, up-all-night visitors, Hadiboh Airport is, as you would expect, very small. If you had a window seat on the plane you'll have enjoyed your first glimpse of Socotra's coastline and possibly the Haggeher Mountains and even the watery curve of Detwah lagoon, so you will be psyched up for this very special trip. In the arrivals hall there's the usual kind of airport chaos but it's good-humoured, luggage gets to the carousel quite quickly (perhaps too quickly; we saw a lot of bags falling off the overloaded trailer as it was brought in from the plane), and the reasonably sized planes mean the crowds aren't overwhelming. That said, paperwork gets matched up manually and immigration can be a bit slow, so don't spend too long taking photos in front of the bottle tree you'll pass by on the walk in from the plane, only to find yourself at the back of the queue. You may see local people greeting each other by touching noses; the custom is to do this up to three times, possibly accompanied by a clicking sound. A child or someone who wishes to show respect to an elder will press their nose on the back of the respected elder's hand. Someone from your local tour operator should meet you in the arrivals hall and take you through to your vehicle.

Driving to Hadiboh is a mixed pleasure. You'll see your first bottle trees on a hillside, and also the abundant, beautiful and very tame Egyptian vultures (page 76). The road runs mostly on flat terrain but then has been cut through an impressively sheer amount of rock, which was hazardous for camels in the days before wheeled transport took over. Hadiboh's serious rubbish problem (page 83) is in evidence here, too: as you approach the town the accumulations of plastic – bottles, bags, discarded toys and other stuff – become more frequent, confirming that Hadiboh is not a pristine jewel in Socotra's crown.

The world's vultures do a fine job of clearing up dead animal bodies and reducing the smell of rural garbage pits by scavenging putrefying matter. Their skill and grace in the air should also astonish anyone who sees them fly. But with their hunched backs, bald pink heads and wrinkled necks, they are ugly! In Africa, they gather on the surrounding walls of outdoor abattoirs and stare down lugubriously into the killing arena, like vultures in animated movies where they are usually scary portents of death.

Imagine our delight then in finding that the Egyptian vultures in Socotra had golden heads. They are still bald of course, allowing them to rummage in animals' innards without getting clotted head feathers that are impossible to preen, but feathers do grow from the crown of the head and down the back of the neck giving them an ageing hippy look. Their plumage, apart from black flight feathers, is stained by the earth to a peach colour. Their resulting resemblance to domestic fowl has obviously been observed before, and they have sometimes been nicknamed Pharaoh's chickens. The birds' rather shy approach to our outdoor table at mealtimes completed their benign image – I have often felt more intimidated by gulls targeting my bag of chips at Skegness.

They do have a sharp curved beak though, and you know they would not hesitate to finish you off if you were lying seriously incapacitated in a ravine. Pharaoh's chickens are still scavengers, and predators of small animals, but earn my admiration for looking good while carrying out their gruesome, but essential, role in the ecosystem.

HADIBOH

As capitals go, Hadiboh (also spelt Hadibo or Hadibu, and pronounced Ha-*dee*-boh with the stress on the middle syllable) is tiny, with around 15,000 inhabitants, a number currently being swelled by incomers from mainland Yemen and adjacent countries who either are escaping Yemen's civil war or see Socotra as an economic opportunity. Some Bedouin communities in more exposed areas have also been relocating due to serious flooding of their villages during recent typhoons. This combination has led to a huge amount of construction in and around the town – parts of it resemble a messy building site – and its size and shape are continuing to change rapidly. Cupped as it is by hills on its inland side and bounded by the sea to the north, expansion will not be easy.

Hadiboh has not been Socotra's capital continuously. In the 1st century BC (if the historic interpretations of its and Socotra's names are correct) it was clearly an important centre, at that time known as Tamara, and, according to Diodorus of Sicily, had a Greek temple of Jupiter that was built with wealth from the aromatics trade. However, what is now the small neighbouring village of Suq (or Shik in Socotri; page 85) then seems to have overtaken it in importance sometime before the 15th century, possibly because Suq's harbour area was more accommodating to shipping. Finally, after the departure of the Portuguese in 1511, Tamara (later to be known as Tamarida, which is how you may see it on old maps, and eventually as Hadiboh) regained – and has kept – its dominance.

For visitors, the active centre of the town is conveniently small. Start at the Grand Mosque – a good, visible landmark – and you're within a few minutes' walking distance of the town's five hotels, banks for foreign exchange, the outdoor fish and

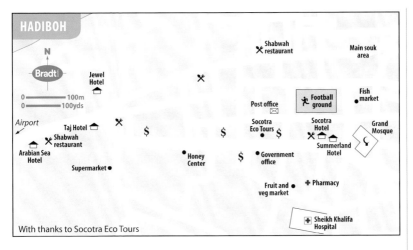

With thanks to Socotra Eco Tours

vegetable markets, the main 'souk' area with a number of small shops selling food, material, clothing, household and electrical goods etc, a pharmacy, some small restaurants with reliably available fish and – should you need it – the Sheik Khalifa Hospital. If you happen to be in town while there is a football game on, they can be very lively affairs, and well worth a look even if you don't particularly enjoy football. Beyond that there's little you will want or need to seek out, except as part of a rather noisy and rubbish-filled general stroll during which, as well as the colourful doors, you should also look at the stonework and tiling on the larger buildings – some are plain but others have intricate patterns and mosaics, giving unexpected little flashes of beauty. In some new buildings too, whether in Hadiboh or elsewhere, the natural colours of the stone (which is quarried on the island) have been carefully chosen to blend together pleasingly. Street names are generally not used; if you need to ask directions, use the Grand Mosque or the Summerland Hotel as landmarks.

🛏 **WHERE TO STAY AND EAT** Hotel bookings will be handled by your tour operator, sometimes even at the last minute if your plans end up changing during your trip. The best hotel in town – the **Summerland**, a simple but clean and pleasant place with a central courtyard, roof terraces, not entirely reliable hot water and a good buffet breakfast – is in biggest demand and can sometimes get filled without notice by visiting VIPs, in which case tourist bookings may well not be honoured and rooms have quickly to be found in the other hotels. Of those, the **Taj** and the **Socotra** have been around for some time while the **Arabian Sea** and the **Jewel** are the newest additions; they are all much of a muchness, serviceable enough and reasonably clean, but with erratic (or no) hot water and possible power cuts. Thanks to Starlink they do tend to offer Wi-Fi these days, but the coverage isn't always the best and you might need to be in a common area to receive it rather than your room. You may need to ask for niceties such as towels and toilet paper – or they may have smartened up their acts by the time you read this. Staff are generally helpful but may not speak much English. A few miles east of Hadiboh is **La Sirena**, a new higher-end hotel with good facilities, Wi-Fi and even a gym! To the West of Hadiboh, directly opposite the airport, is the relatively new (and rather amusingly named) **Heathrow Hotel**, offering container-style cabins at a comparable price to hotel rooms in Hadiboh. While there isn't a whole lot to see or do by foot near here, it's obviously very convenient if you have an early flight the next day. 🛏

1

1–6 Hadiboh will never win a beauty contest — its rubbish-strewn streets are prone to flooding, and the buildings are crumbling and dilapidated. But here you will find a busy market selling fruit, vegetables and the catch of the day, flashes of colour in the metal doors, a chance to stock up on supplies for the adventure ahead and — above all — a warm Socotri welcome.

2

1 Chris Miller, 2 Nicole Smoot; 3 Simon Urwin, 4 & 6 Nicole Smoot, 5 Chris Miller

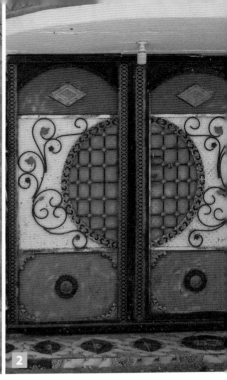

1–4   The people of both Hadiboh and Qalansiyah take great pride in their colourful doors, made by local craftsmen.

1 Nicole Smoot, 2,3 & 4 Chris Miller

Hadiboh: unlovely capital of a magical island. As you approach Hadiboh from Socotra's miniature airport, or from any other direction, a harbinger of rubbish begins to make its presence felt. You wait for the rubbish to lessen as you get nearer to the centre but it only increases, as does the multitude of free-range goats. Encircled by the rubbish, public and private buildings are mostly made crudely from concrete blocks with flat roofs. Exceptionally you pass mosques of some elegance which kick this trend of concrete and flat roofs and you marvel at the sanctuary offered by the Summerland Hotel with its two storeys of rooms looking on to a tranquil courtyard. We loved this haven.

Even when buildings have some distinction and show signs of having interiors which are clean and tidy, there is no *cordon sanitaire* as you step out into the street: rubbish throttles the buildings.

And yet there is one endearing feature: the people of Hadiboh and the island's second town, Qalansiyah, take great pride in their front doors. These are mostly made of metal in a variety of colours and often charming filigree. Many buildings have them and new ones are lined up in the rubble-strewn streets for sale. It is a credit to these doors and their owners that their decorative charm rises triumphantly above the tide of rubbish.

Restaurants are small, simple and becoming increasingly used to foreigners; menus aren't extensive but food can be quite good. The Shabwah is generally the one tourists are taken to, and has recently opened a second branch near the Arabian Sea hotel, but the others shown on the map are fine too. (The one next to the Socotra hotel shakes up a tasty fruit smoothie.) Your guide will advise you. Also see *Eating and drinking*, page 66.

SHOPPING It's easy in Hadiboh because the centre is so small. Just browse, from shop to shop. The **Honey Center** in the main street sells (when it hasn't run out of stock, which happens) a good selection of Socotran honey, well displayed, and some other souvenirs. Members of the **Socotra Women's Association** make and sell handicrafts (bags, baskets, woven items, jewellery, hats, pottery, clothing…) and are well worth supporting. Your guide might also take you to the outdoor **fish market**, round the corner from the Summerland Hotel, which has fish sellers hacking away at various species, large and small, as well as a few stalls selling vegetables, honey, dates etc. Near the hospital there's another colourful **fruit and vegetable market** that has recently opened, too. If you fancy some home-grown tomatoes, try **Mona's Garden** (page 89), an interesting small plant- and tree-conservation project just outside the town.

On the southern edge of Hadiboh you can also visit the **Ma'anhifah Community Gardens** (⊕ 12°37'51.6"N 54°02'13.0"E), managed by a collective of over 100 women. They grow a wide range of fruits and vegetables and are happy to show you around. A donation to support their gardens, preferably in local currency, will be highly appreciated. Close to the community gardens is the **Delfadehin Pottery Association** (⊕ 12°37'22.1"N 54°01'48.8"E). This is a great place to see the women demonstrate how they painstakingly make their local pottery by hand (page 69). As with the gardens, any donation will be much appreciated after you have been shown their craft.

See also, *Shopping*, page 68.

1 A small lagoon near Hawlaf (page 86) (Chris Miller)

2 The Ghubbah Sinkhole is located just off the main road, midway between Hadiboh and Qalansiyah (page 90)
(Chris Miller)

EAST OF HADIBOH

SUQ VILLAGE Known in Socotri as Shiq, and the island's capital or main town for some centuries until Hadiboh overtook it, this small village a couple of miles east of Hadiboh (not particularly striking today) played a brief but showy role in Socotra's history. In April 1506 the Portuguese, as part of a larger endeavour to thwart Muslim trade in the Indian Ocean, dispatched 16 ships from Lisbon to capture what they had heard was a strategically useful island where, although it was mainly under Arab rule, Christianity was still practised. After a year-long voyage, the fleet – under the overall command of Tristan da Cunha – finally reached Socotra and landed at Suq in April 1507. A local force of around 130 men awaited them and defended Suq's sturdy Arab fortress fiercely in a battle lasting several days. Standing in the small town today, it is hard to imagine the bay crowded with 16 fighting ships, and the noise of medieval warfare. Eventually the Portuguese claimed victory, negotiated a peace treaty which included a tribute in goats from the population, and took over the fortress, believed to be the one whose (sparse) ruin is on the hill to the east of the village, renaming it San Miguel. Da Cunha continued to India, leaving behind a 100-strong garrison. San Miguel's battle-damage was repaired, and a mosque in the village (it is said) became the Church of Our Lady of Victory.

Socotra's inhabitants took a poor view of their conquerors, however, harassing them with repeated attacks and a consistent lack of cooperation until, after only four years, the Portuguese decided to cut their losses and quit. Early in 1511 they sent two ships to Socotra with orders to raze San Miguel and evacuate its garrison, together with any Christians who wanted to leave. Although Socotra then reverted (temporarily) to Arab rule, Portuguese ships continued to call in, welcomed more warmly by the islanders as traders than they had been as conquerors. Suq began to diminish – and Hadiboh to increase – in importance, and there is an unconfirmed theory that Suq's shoreline may subsequently have shifted so that it provided less convenient anchorage.

Today if you climb up to the supposed ruin of the fortress there's a good view back along the coast towards Hadiboh, otherwise Suq has little of visible interest apart from the very visitable tree nursery described below.

The Adeeb Tree Nursery

We visited this family-run tree nursery because its creator's son, Ahmed, was our driver for the first two days. He told us how it had been set up by his father, Adeeb Hadid, with help from the Edinburgh Botanical Gardens where Ahmed went for training as a botanist – 'but there's no work now for botanists.' When his father started the nursery in 1996 there was plenty of government help, and it was supported by the Socotra Conservation Development Project (SCDP); 'He planted 100 dragon's blood seeds and only one grew,' Ahmed told us, 'but a week later another one came up, and then another, until we had a big collection. And then the government withdrew their help.' Ahmed continues taking care of the saplings, against the odds, but there is no government assistance and reintroducing the young trees to their natural habitat would be a big undertaking (it is being done by other nurseries, near Diksam and Firmihin, however – pages 121 and 117). The spiky baby dragons look like sisal: hard to believe they grow into those characteristic umbrellas that stand sentinel over Socotra's landscapes. It is only after about 12 years that they are tall and mature enough to be replanted, because then the leaves are no longer palatable to goats.

The nursery also has most of the frankincense tree species, and many other endemics including the pretty relative to the pomegranate, *Punica protopunica*. All

The indigenous people of Socotra were actively engaged for millennia in producing rock art visible at four main sites across the island, three of which can be found in this area: Eriosh, Deda'ahneten and Delisha. These three sites can be easily visited, seen and photographed, but do please refrain from walking on or rubbing the motifs so that they can be preserved for future generations. Further information on these and other rock art on Socotra can be found at w socotraculturalheritage. org/rock-art. For the fourth site, Hoq Cave, see page 108.

ERIOSH This open-air rock art site is approximately 20km southwest of Hadiboh and 500m south of the village of Alm⁻ah. It measures approximately 10,000m² (1ha) and can be easily accessed from the road, which sadly was built across part of it in 2003. The site consists of a flat limestone plain; after the rains of the monsoon period, much of it is covered by water which is used locally to water livestock. Petroglyphs can be found across the entire site, although they are densest towards the central part. Here one can find motifs of feet, singularly and in pairs; crosses; geometric patterns; an ancient script; and figures of humans and animals that include camels, snakes and an abstract horned animal believed to be a goat. The protected site is now considered to have been used continuously by the indigenous people of Socotra for several millennia, charting their social, religious and economic lives. Some 655 motifs have been recorded in total, which represent some of the earliest art to be found on the island.

DEDA'AHNETEN This open-air rock art site, about 350m southwest of Suq and 2.5km east of Hadiboh, measures approximately 176m in length and is the first

of them are cared for by volunteers. Will the island's administration ever be stable enough – and concerned enough – to support this project? Who knows, but it will provide you with a good introduction to the island's endemic plants before you set out to see them *in situ*, and visits by tour groups would give the work a useful boost.

The nursery is on the inland side of the main coast road about 2 miles east of Hadiboh. It isn't signposted but ⊕ 12°39'51.3"N 54°03'04.3"E should take you there. Ask your guide to check beforehand that it will be open.

HAWLAF (HULAF, HAULAF) The sudden stretch of dual carriageway as you drive eastward from Hadiboh marks the entrance to Socotra's recently redeveloped **port**, by the village of Hawlaf just beyond Suq, where a lot of construction work is still under way at present. It was inaugurated in 2018. You'll see cranes, containers, warehouses and so forth as you drive by, and it's a reminder of how dependent the island is, for supplies, on shipping and the few flights from the mainland. Best not to take photos here (it's not attractive anyway), particularly if there's any sort of military presence in evidence. On a stretch of beach just beyond the port is a new campsite with caravans to stay in; a popular spot due to its proximity to Hadiboh and Delisha. The high headland beyond is Ras Hawlaf (or Riy Di Hawlaf).

DELISHA It's attractive, it's a convenient 30-minute drive east from Hadiboh, and while it looks tempting for swimming, there can be ferociously strong currents here. Pay attention if your guide advises you it's unsafe to swim, as a tourist drowned off this beach in recent years after ignoring advice from the locals. There

cultural heritage site to be officially protected on Socotra, so please note that walking on or rubbing the motifs is a punishable offence. Petroglyphs can be found across the entire site, although the majority are within the central area. Here one can find motifs that include feet, cupules (small cup-like shapes), a ship, various geometric patterns, cruciform shapes, several plant-like images and an ancient script. This script is similar to that found at Eriosh and, according to archaeologists, belongs to the family of ancient South Semitic scripts although, as of yet, it remains undeciphered. Much like Eriosh, this site provides us with a record of Socotra's history up until arguably the 16th century, when the Portuguese came to the island.

DELISHA The site of Delisha is technically not rock art but stone markers. There are four large stones and one fragment, all of which have been inscribed by Gujarati visitors and merchants who visited Socotra around the 17th and 18th century. These stones tell the story of Gujarati sailors and merchants who sailed to this port and spent several months on the island, and gives details about their journeys, their routes to and from Socotra and the names of the people on board. What makes these stones so important is that up until recently there has been little direct evidence for Indian merchants and seafarers having been engaged in the Indian Ocean trade or having visited Socotra. Now, not only do we have this evidence, but we are given a completely new perspective on the role of Indian merchants in this trade, and their links with what was known by them as *sīkhotara* (Socotra). To find this site, just go into Delisha village and ask for someone to show you. Expect to pay a small fee.

is a new eco-lodge here with good food on offer. The lodge has attractive dome huts coated in washed-up coral. The huts have beds, electricity and even air-con, however the washroom facilities are shared. When Chris and Miranda visited in March 2024 the friendly owner, Abdul Rahman, was in the process of building more huts and facilities. Another hotel was also being built nearby with an eye-catching colourful plastic playground in the middle. This is good location to base yourself and visit the northeast of the island if you prefer not to be camping. It also offers good protection in the windy season when other campsites in the area are untenable. Plus, there's an impressive giant sand dune which the energetic can climb and slide down. The claim that it was called Delisha because someone exclaimed 'It's delicious!' might be a touch fanciful, however. Ernst Haeckel (1834–1919), the exhaustingly prolific German biologist, naturalist, evolutionist, artist, philosopher and doctor who spent his life researching and illustrating flora and fauna, sailed past the northern coast on 18 March 1882: his highly stylised painting of a sand dune with the same date is most probably Delisha. He describes 'the picturesque coast of Socotra, where the ravines are marked by immense fields of snow-white sand, looking like glaciers sloping to the sea.' Nearby Delisha village has an important archaeological site; see above.

WEST OF HADIBOH

QADHEB Driving westward along the coast from Hadiboh, before the airport you come to this small, traditional **fishing village**. It is less interesting in itself than for

Dr Kay Van Damme

For decades, many different organisations have supported nature conservation in the Socotra archipelago. However, such grassroots initiatives succeed only when they are requested, implemented and maintained by local communities or individuals. Several such exist on Socotra; these are two examples that you could ask your guide to arrange for you to visit, as interest from tourists and appreciation of their work will give such a boost to the people involved.

MANGROVE REPLANTATION PLOT IN GHUBBAH Just a few years ago in the small village of Ghubbah, about half an hour's drive westward from Hadiboh, the local community created a unique Socotri NGO called the **Al Tamek Association for the Protection of the Mangrove Tree**. Within living memory of the village elders, stands of grey mangrove (*Avicennia marina*) still occurred in a few areas along Socotra's north coast, remnants of a larger abundance in different parts of the island over a century ago. Now, however, the old stands have all disappeared along the north coast, and tiny patches remain in only two small nature sanctuaries in the southwest. The 2015 cyclones had a devastating impact on stands in the south. Mangrove ecosystems have great importance worldwide – they act as productive fish nurseries, help protect against coastal erosion, and are valuable blue carbon sinks (carbon stored in coastal ecosystems). In Socotra, they are considered as aesthetic, producing valuable wood, and play an important role in the local folklore and culture. In 2017, by direct request from the Al Tamek Association, the charity Friends of Soqotra joined with the Arab Regional Centre for World Heritage and the Environmental Protection Agency in Socotra to implement the **Mangrove Ecosystem Restoration and Mitigation of Cyclone Impact** project. Its objective was to replant mangrove seedlings in Ghubbah, derived from the surviving stands in the southwest. The Al Tamek Association's contribution, in a joint effort with local fishermen, children and teachers, was to protect the tiny mangrove trees from being eaten by crabs, and to build a strong fence to keep goats out. By 2019, over 80 mangrove plants, some already producing their own seeds, were growing

the adjacent **lagoon**: a beautiful and peaceful spot for birdwatching, with various wading birds and even flamingos at times. To the east of the village are some **old cave dwellings**, part of the original village and now disused.

Qadheb used to be dangerously prone to flooding; many homes were destroyed in 1998, and again in 2004, by water surging down the wadi and through the village on its way to the sea. In 2006 the UNDP Small Grants Programme was asked to provide funds and the villagers pitched in to clear land and build protective banks and barriers of stones strongly encased in wire mesh, so that – a simple solution – future floods could be routed safely down the resulting channel and away from the dwellings. With a lot of stone to shift, it was heavy work, but the result was visibly satisfactory.

AYHAFT CANYON NATIONAL PARK The fact that the turn-off to this botanical treasure-house is relatively near the airport makes it often the first stop on an itinerary. The distance is deceptive, because the main coast road is much faster

in what is the first successful mangrove nursery in the wild on Socotra's north coast. To the great pride of Ghubbah's population, the small trees are healthy, growing near huge ancient fallen mangrove trunks that recall the north coast's once majestic trees. The project demonstrates what can be achieved when communities, local government and international organisations communicate and cooperate together.

If you would like to see some beautiful small mangrove trees and meet the kind people of Ghubbah, ask your guide to contact the Al Tamek Association to arrange a visit. The Chairperson is Saleh Ahmed Abdullah Jam'an. On arrival you should go to the main village first (⊕ 12°37'04.9"N 53°45'46.3"E), where someone will take you to the mangrove site.

MONA AHMED ABUBAKAR'S GARDEN NEAR HADIBOH An individual replanting initiative, near Hadiboh, is the brainchild of an enthusiastic, skilful and nature-loving Socotri woman named **Mona Ahmed Abubakar**. Initially she just grew tomatoes but now uses her garden, which is well protected against goats, to plant local trees. This approach – agroforestry (or combining gardening with the protection of trees) – is sustainable, as the local community passes on these small gardens to future generations. **Mona's Garden** has several tree species from the direct vicinity, such as *Boswellia elongata* and *Commiphora ornifolia*. Socotra's much-loved *Boswellia* (frankincense trees) suffer in the same way as dragon's blood trees from the island's fierce climate and ever-hungry goats, and Mona's is one of several local projects to protect them. She is well known on the island, and kind, distributing tomato seeds and seedlings to the community. Since 2006 she has worked with Czech researchers to grow seedlings of various unique local species for nearby reforestation, and is now helping to coordinate seed germination trials on Socotra for several *Boswellia* species.

Mona's Garden is in Qishn, about 2km east of Hadiboh town (⊕ 12°38'30.6"N 54°02'27.4"E). If you would like to visit, ask your guide to arrange it with Mona in advance – and if you want to buy some fresh tomatoes too, check their availability. For details of another successful female gardener also planting *Boswellia*, near Qalansiyah, see **Aziza Said Fadnhan's garden** (page 138).

than the stretch after the turn-off, but it is very well worth a visit: the sight of desert roses (bottle trees) perhaps in flower, cucumber trees and other endemic plant life – along with various birds including, if you're lucky, the Socotra sparrow, Socotra sunbird and both Socotra and Somali starlings – all set against a spectacular mountain backdrop is irresistible, and a dramatic introduction to Socotra. There is also a dammed pool of cold, clear water here which looks enticing for a swim *but* this is the local population's drinking water so understandably they are not keen on tourists cavorting in it. Better to wait for the natural pools in the various wadis you will visit later. However, in and around the stream you can make your first acquaintance with one of the colourful endemic Socotran freshwater crabs, the rather charmingly named *Socotrapotamon socotrensis*.

There is a camping area near the end of the canyon's access road (⊕ 12°36'38.4" N 53°58'37.1"E) located in a wide area of valley with small streams on either side, and surrounded by views of the rugged Haggeher Mountains. It's beautifully quiet in the evening apart from the hooting of the Socotra scops owl, which if you're lucky you may even be able to see. The site had no bathroom facilities at the time of writing this edition.

Ayhaft Canyon to Hadiboh Hike *(8km; 5hrs inc stops)*

Rather than drive back out of Ayhaft, it's possible to hike up to the ridge near the top of the canyon and then down towards Hadiboh via Hazerh di Meqaderhan Valley, where your driver can pick you up again. The hike takes around 5 hours in total, split fairly evenly between going up and then down. The first part of the hike is the steepest, so it's best to camp overnight then get up early to pack your tents and set off, thereby avoiding the heat of the sun for this section. The vegetation is denser here than almost anywhere else you'll visit on Socotra, and it is a fantastic route for spotting endemic birds, trees and succulents. If you are lucky you can find the Socotra white-eye, sunbird, shrike and golden-winged grosbeak here. At the top of the canyon on the steeper rocks and cliffs you can see a noticeable number of young dragon's blood trees, safely out of reach of the grazing goats. Socotra figs (*Dorstenia gigas*) can also be spotted growing impossibly out of the rocky crevices with bright orange blooms when in flowering season. The descent down the valley towards Hadiboh (where your driver will be waiting somewhere below) follows a bouldered path, with expansive and picturesque views of Hadiboh and the north coast stretching out in front of you.

GHUBBAH SINKHOLE   Continuing west along the main road towards Qalansiyah you'll see (and likely stop to photograph) some old Soviet tanks lined up along the shoreline. Shortly past these is the village of Ghubbah where there is a large cenote (sinkhole), about 45m across and nearly 40m deep (⊕ 12°36'29.7"N 53°47'06.1"E). The local children here will likely take great delight in showing you their jumps and flips into this remarkably deep pool.

GHUBBAH CRATER   About 1km past the sinkhole, and shortly before the left-hand turn on to the cross-country route to Shu'ab (⊕ 12°35'45.3"N 53°46'40.0"E), is a sizable water-filled crater which some claim was made by a meteorite (or it could be a sinkhole). You can scramble down to the water's edge and walk around. A few birds come to drink and small-scale salt-making is carried out – as it apparently was in 1834 when Lieutenant James Wellsted made his survey of the island, since he marked the place 'salt' on the sketch map that he drew. There are also some places along the shore where pans have been dug and salt is collected; see photo on page 38.

JOURNEY BOOKS

CONTRACT PUBLISHING FROM BRADT GUIDES

DO YOU HAVE A STORY TO TELL?

- Publish your book with a leading trade publisher
- Expert management of your book by our experienced editors
- Professional layout, cover design and printing
- <u>Unique</u> access to trade distribution for print books and ebooks
- Competitive pricing and a range of tailor-made packages
- Aimed at both first-timers and previously published authors

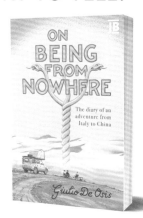

"Unfailingly pleasant"... "Undoubtedly one of the best publishers I have worked with"... "Excellent and incredibly prompt communication"... "Unfailingly courteous"... "Superb"...

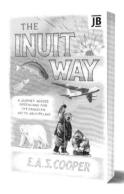

For more information – and many more endorsements from our delighted authors – please visit: **bradtguides.com/journeybooks.**

Journey Books is the contract publishing imprint of award-winning travel publisher, Bradt Guides. All subjects are considered for Journey Books, not just travel. Our contract publishing is a complement to our traditional publishing, not a replacement, and we welcome traditional submissions from new and established travel writers. Please visit bradtguides.com/write-for-us to find out more.

4

The East

There are…many perennial streams on the island, especially in the central granite region, where amongst the hills the most charming bubbling burns dashing over boulders in a series of cascades, or purling gently over a pebbling shingle, make it hard to believe that one is in such proximity to the desert region of Arabia.

Isaac Bayley Balfour, *Botany of Socotra*, 1880

Of all tourist areas in Socotra, this is the one that packs the most attractions into a relatively small space. You have birds, snorkelling, massive sand dunes, inland pastures, Socotra's only museum, Hoq Cave, dragon's blood and bottle trees, a meeting point between two oceans and some superb freshwater swimming pools – and you should sleep very well at the end of your explorations!

The storm-swept eastern promontory and the reefs around it have seen many shipwrecks over the centuries and looted objects have found their way into several local homes. A strictly un-lootable item, in 1887, was a fully grown tiger, being carried from India to Berlin Zoo by the German passenger liner SS *Oder I* when she was wrecked. Fortunately for the villagers but unfortunately for the tiger, despite escaping from its cage it then stayed on board rather than swimming ashore, and so starved to death.

PROTECTED AREAS

All along the shoreline of the coast covered in this chapter, for about 2–3km stretching outward from the shore, the sea fringing the coast is designated a '**national park**' within the terms of the archipelago's Conservation Zoning Plan, set up by Presidential Decree in 2000 (page 163). This categorisation defines what the area can be used for. Under the Zoning Plan, a 'national park' is:

…a natural area of land or sea designated to protect the ecological integrity of the unique ecosystems of Socotra islands for present and future generations to provide a foundation for scientific, educational, and recreational opportunities, beside the appropriate development activities for ecotourism…To perpetuate representative examples of the unique biotic communities, genetic resources, and endemic species, found in the Socotra islands, and maintain biodiversity. To manage these areas in a sound environmental manner for educational, cultural and recreational purposes.

Other stretches of the archipelago's shoreline are similarly designated and also have protective belts; this is the longest stretch on Socotra itself, running from just east of Hawlaf port near Hadiboh to the southern edge of Ras Erissel peninsula, but the other three islands (page 152) are completely encircled.

The text of the Conservation Zoning Plan plus maps showing the locations of the various categories can be found on the Socotra Project's website, w socotraproject. org/userfiles/files/Zoning%20plan%20information.pdf.

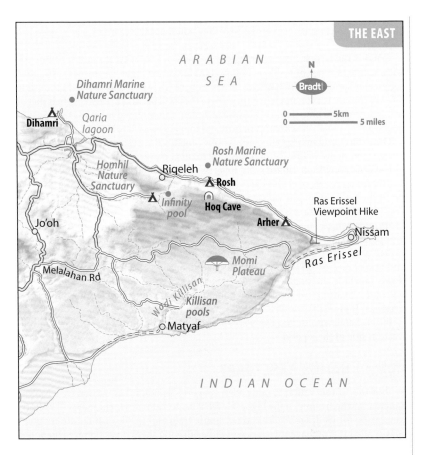

ARABIAN
SEA

Dihamri Marine
Nature Sanctuary

Dihamri

Qaria
lagoon

N

Bradt

0 ———— 5km
0 ———— 5 miles

Rosh Marine
Nature Sanctuary

Homhil
Nature
Sanctuary

Riqeleh

Rosh

Infinity
pool

Hoq Cave

Ras Erissel
Viewpoint Hike

Jo'oh

Arher

Nissam

Melalahan Rd

Momi
Plateau

Ras Erissel

Wadi Killisan

Killisan
pools

Matyaf

INDIAN OCEAN

Within the 'national park' category, there are smaller and more ecologically fragile areas of land or sea with higher protected status designated '**nature sanctuaries**'. These are described as:

> …areas of land or sea characterized by rare plant or animal species still retaining their natural character set aside for scientific research whose objective is to preserve rare and fragile habitats, ecosystems, species and unique landscapes in as undisturbed a state as possible. To maintain the essential natural attributes and qualities of the environment over the long term for future generations.

In this chapter, the three nature sanctuaries are **Rosh** and **Dihamri marine nature sanctuaries** and the **Homhil** area.

QARIA LAGOON

About 30km east of Hadiboh, opposite the turnoff to Dihamri is Qaria lagoon, a Y-shaped body of water which is a favourite lunch stop before turning off the main coastal road and taking the mountainous route to Homhil. Vultures know about the lunch stop, and start discreetly getting into position when vehicles arrive; they keep their distance and are entertaining to watch. One writer with a shaky grasp of English explained that they 'often eat the remnants of visitors', so take care!

Qaria is the largest freshwater lagoon in Socotra and of great interest to birders, with a large number of resident and migrant birds seen here. Of the latter you may see greater flamingos which spend the winter here. They probably breed on the saline lakes of Iran or Turkey and when they arrive they will be pink because of their diet of brine shrimp and blue-green algae which contain the natural dye canthaxanthin. On Socotra they mostly lose their pinkness and may appear white or grey.

Other birds you may spot include herons (notably the western reef heron and grey heron), and many wading birds, especially Kentish plovers, sand plovers, little stints, greenshank and black-winged stilts. Kestrels nest on the surrounding rocky cliffs.

The road crosses over the narrowest part of the lagoon, and on the short walk up to the view point you will see quite a few endemic plants in this characteristic croton shrubland (page 5), including the eponymous species of Euphorbia, *Croton socotranus*, which is common on the coastal plains. It has many local uses, being a popular browse for goats, and important for Socotra's honey business since its nectar produces particularly good honey without a trace of bitterness. The trunk and branches are also used extensively by the locals as roofing material. Endemic flowers include the pretty purple Persian violet (*Exacum affine*), and *Oldenlandia pulvinata*, an attractive and fragrant endemic, which is often fed to milk-producing livestock. It gives their milk a distinctively sweet flavour.

From the viewpoint you can also see the houses of nearby Qaria village, on the western side of the lagoon.

HOMHIL NATURE SANCTUARY

Within the Conservation Zoning Plan (page 163) Homhil is classed as a Nature Sanctuary, which allows it the highest level of protection. It is included in all visitors' itineraries, for its dragon's blood trees, bottle trees and the beautiful 'infinity pool' as we called it. You have the choice of either driving there or walking, depending on the time available and the fitness (and age) of your group.

The driving route starts just beyond Qaria, where one of two roads will take you up into the mountains. Should you take the older road of the two, you will understand why virtually all the vehicles in Socotra are four-wheel drive. Your jeep will splash through streams, be hauled round hairpin bends, and roar up steep inclines. The newer road was recently built by Saudi Arabia and is somewhat easier going. We suggest taking the new road up and the old road down, should you be returning back the same way. Regardless of route, if this is your initial day you will see your first dragon's blood trees, all shapes and sizes of bottle trees, *Boswellia* frankincense trees along with cucumber trees and feel that you are well and truly in otherworldly Socotra. In contrast to the coastal plain that you have just left, this is a weirder, greener landscape. You pass eroded pink limestone rocks, including one huge one if you travel the old road, pleated by the elements, with a cave at its base which has been turned into a dwelling by a retaining wall. If you are in one vehicle, rather than a convoy, you will find yourself stopping frequently to take photos, and in a convoy you should arrange beforehand that the lead vehicle will stop from time to time at viewpoints when the road is safe.

The walk up takes you directly to the infinity pool (see opposite), and begins about 15km from Qaria at a small village just off the main coastal road. The climb takes between 1 and 2 hours, depending on the age and fitness of the group, and it is worth taking your time for the many geckos and invertebrates to spot and photograph.

Nicole (page vi), who was with a group of differing abilities, describes the climb: 'It took us about 2 hours to reach the pool from the north. You pass plenty of endemic plants – on the first flat section lots of Jatropha and croton trees. The next section starts meandering up the base of the cliff, still among the Jatropha and some croton, and the occasional bottle tree. As it gets steeper the bottle trees are more numerous and you'll start getting better views of the Arabian Sea. At the end of that section, you'll reach an overhanging rock face that makes for a good rest point with shade. The last bit is a somewhat steep hike. You'll pass one young dragon's blood tree just as you get above the rock face where the views are outstanding. After climbing about 300m, you emerge over a ridge and suddenly there is Homhil and the infinity pool.'

The campsite has a basic bathroom, a cooking area and a couple of shelters. It can get quite popular, however, and there's not a lot of space for tents, so it's not unusual to see groups camping further down below the car park, where there is a lot more room – but also no bathroom facilities. Emily Glover points out that in Socotra, 'there are traces of history if you know how to look. My favourite spot for thinking of Socotra's human story was at Homhil. Close to a site called Seiyun you will find a wonderful, manmade worn-stone lined spring. It is home to a population of rare endemic Socotri freshwater crabs – a sight in itself.'

From the campsite, or the end of the hike up, you will be guided to the **infinity pool**, which many of our group would agree was their favourite place on the whole island; the walk there is quintessential Socotra in all its beauty and weirdness. A faint

SO MUCH VARIETY, SO MANY SURPRISES   *Oona Muirhead*

One of the magical aspects of Socotra is how such a small landmass can hold such a huge variety of different landscapes. It's the equivalent of the surreal mix of architecture you find walking through the city of London: a tiny Renaissance church with green bird-filled garden nestling against a 25-storey, glass-fronted example of modernity.

The walk from our camp at Homhil was our first experience of finding that every corner you turn in Socotra holds a hidden surprise. A rocky but well-defined trail around the contour of the hill gave views across the narrow valley to hilly uplands with the occasional majestic dragon's blood tree – regular and ordered in shape as though all cut from a single template. It was such a contrast to the delightfully unique bottle trees we passed on our side of the valley – some smaller ones sprouting improbably from what looked like solid rock, their little toes clenched; others bigger, like those mid-size wind-turbines with a huge body and tiny arms. But all with such charming postures and unique shapes that you instantly fell in love with them as though sentient beings. I confess to succumbing to the occasional hug with a tree: there's something about bottles that instantly captures the heart. Pausing to photograph almost each and every one, you had to take care a gust of wind flying up from the sea didn't knock you to the stony ground, and I was more than once grateful to our watchful drivers for lending an arm. All the while being buffeted the sun kissed us out of a blue, blue sky, and – when we turned another corner – shone on to a sparkling turquoise natural 'infinity pool' silhouetted against the white-capped sea beyond. The path took us down a couple of hundred metres of solid reddish-coloured rock which I could imagine in the rainy season would be like a water slide. Emerging refreshed from the pool, the wind that had felt so exhilaratingly gusty now dried us almost instantly, like a Dyson hair drier.

path takes you along a narrow bed of salmon-pink limestone, with a stream on your left backed by a high cliff and mountain peaks ahead. Squished between the rocks or clinging to the sides of them are bottle trees, and it's hard not to get anthropomorphic about them when so many are reminiscent of buttocks or bellies (see photos, pages 8 and 10). Scattered around or silhouetted on the horizon are dragon's blood trees like giant mushrooms, and ahead, cradled in a limestone hollow on the brink of a precipice and fed by a small waterfall, lies a deep pool of clear water, the infinity pool. It's cool for swimming, but not cold, and even has its own rather bumpy water chute, on a sloping strip of flat rock. Liz Lea commented: 'While we were swimming we were taken by surprise by a local woman appearing suddenly and diving into the pool in a full niqab! Did she have a change of clothing, we wondered?' Every visitor will come here and the danger is that it'll get overcrowded. But that's the way it is with any spectacular tourist – and local – attraction. It's rough walking – you need shoes with gripping soles or even boots and we were grateful for our hiking poles for balance. Despite it only being about a kilometre from the campsite, expect the walk to the pool to take longer than you think. The otherworldly landscape here is enthralling and you'll likely stop to admire and photograph many bottle and dragon's blood trees along the way.

MOMI PLATEAU

To the southeast of Homhil, and often an add-on from a visit there, is the Momi Plateau, an area of rolling limestone ridges, red earth and scattered shrubs overlying deep caves of which many are still unexplored. Some contain rare endemic freshwater shrimps and other invertebrates, and the hard-to-access Dahaisi Cave, not currently open to visitors, recently revealed some archaeologically valuable rock art. There is a persistent, age-old belief on Socotra that the island's caves are guarded by a great white snake, and serpents have featured in ancient legends. More recently, there have been accounts of strange sounds and movements in some of the deeper caves.

Visitors come here for the dramatic landscape and abundance of bottle trees, which towards the end of February will be in flower. For those wanting to stretch

---

THE SEVEN STAGES OF – GRASS   *With thanks to Miranda Morris*

Socotra's two main livelihoods are from fishing and pastoralism, and for the Bedouin, with their traditional pattern of transhumance between pastures, **grass** – and the quality of that grass – has always been of great importance. The Socotri language reflects this, with grass's categories carefully described.

Bitil mqanhim   There is enough grass 'to end the need to lop foliage.'
Qerhe ta'amo ḥidibi   'Just enough for local livestock to have a taster.'
Shibo'o dish ḥidibi   'Enough for local livestock to eat their fill.'
Qaṣeho di-irihan: tuw'an dish   'Feed for mature goats: enough for people with small stock to transhume [move their herds] to.'
Qaṣeho di-folihi wa minqo': tuw' an dish   'Feed for weaned calves: enough for people with young cattle to transhume to.'
Qaṣeho di ilehe: tuw' an dish   'Feed for cattle: enough for people with pregnant and milking cows to transhume to.'
Qala' bi chadihir wa 'a iteybur   The highest rangeland quality and 'enough pasture for a clay pot to be thrown to the ground and not break.'

their legs and explore Momi where very few people go, Chris and Miranda's guide Ruslan said that it is possible to hike from Homhil to a hamlet called Arient, a bit less than 6km in total. It's relatively easy going, and a great way to experience the plateau. There is also the chance to drive and then trek down for a dip in deep pools in the Killisan (also spelt Kalisan) canyon (see below), which Nicole describes as 'beautiful turquoise pools surrounded by white rock.' (Ruslan says it's also possible to trek on from Arient through to Killisan. It's about 12km, however, and the route is rather rough going with lots of large boulders and a big canyon to navigate over and through, so takes 6 hours or more.) Plant-wise the plateau is typical succulent shrubland, with the silhouettes of dragon's blood trees against a mountain backdrop. Several Bedouin villages dot the landscape, and ever-hungry goats browse for food.

It is possible to drive through to the south coast from here (or vice versa) via a less visited route known as the Melalahan Road. The literal translation is 'boring road', though it really is anything but. This is a bumpy but beautiful drive, winding its way through picturesque valleys covered with huge numbers of bottle trees, probably more than anywhere else in Socotra. It is especially worthwhile when the bottle trees are in flower as you'll see their pink blooms in every direction. If you stop to walk among them however, beware: there are even more orb-weavers and their huge webs (page 17) here than there are bottle trees. As the drive starts to flatten out towards the southern end, you'll travel along Wadi De Fa'rhu – the perfect place to stop and stretch the legs, or have a picnic and look out for birds and dragonflies.

THE POOLS OF KILLISAN

This spectacular place belongs geographically more to the south but is most easily accessed by vehicle from the Momi Plateau and so is included here. It is one of Socotra's hidden wonders and you need to be prepared to hike from the parking area to get there, but it's absolutely worth it for the series of turquoise pools of water, fed by small waterfalls, set in smooth, white limestone. Nicole writes: 'I've read that Killisan is home to the largest freshwater pool on Socotra. The swimming here is superb and makes for a great relaxed day in the middle of a trip. Wadi Killisan ends on the southern coast at Khor Matyaf, but we accessed it from the southern end of the Momi Plateau, turning off on to a dirt track and then hiking down to the wadi. The hike took about 45 minutes each way along a goat trail that was pretty straightforward but had some loose stones to be wary of. Alternatively, you can access the pools by a 2-hour trek up from Matyaf village on the southern coast road.' If, like most people, you are visiting from the Momi end, there are some containers at the parking area where people often have lunch before or after visiting the pools. We were told it is possible to camp at this location if you really wish to, though given it's still a fair distance from the pools and there's not much more here than a gravel area with no bathroom facilities, it's not something we'd recommend.

Matt from Inertia Network adds: 'It's about a 2-hour drive from the road junction near Dihamri to the start of the trail down to the pools. You can also take a boat from Ras Erissel and hike up the river from there into the wadi. An alternative is to make a two- or three-day trek from Homhil, across the Momi Plateau and down into Wadi Killisan towards the Indian Ocean.'

THE PROTECTED MARINE AREAS

The north coast of Socotra has accessible and protected coral reefs which, like so much in Socotra, are home to some unusual and endemic species, with an overlap between

1 Qaria lagoon, where flamingoes are often seen (page 93) (Chris Miller)

2 Homhil plateau (page 94) (Chris Miller)

3 & 4 Perhaps Socotra's most popular site, this natural pool on Homhil plateau is often referred to as the 'infinity pool' (page 95) (Chris Miller)

5 Some of the scenery on the hills around Homhil (page 94) (Chris Miller)

1 Momi Plateau, to the east of Homhil (page 96)
(Chris Miller)

2 Bottle trees along the scenic Melalahan Road (page 97)
(Chris Miller)

3 Killisan Pools (page 97) (Nicole Smoot)

4 The beach by Rosh Marine Nature Sanctuary is littered
with shells and coral fragments
(page 107) (Hilary Bradt)

5 Dihamri Marine Nature Sanctuary. The best snorkelling
is just offshore between camp and the red pyramid rock
(page 107) (Chris Miller)

Clambering up Arher's biggest sand dune (page 110) (Simon Urwin)

1 Ras Erissel beach at sunset (page 111) (Chris Miller)

2 Whale bones washed up on Ras Erissel beach (Chris Miller)

3 Ras Erissel is a veritable treasure trove for beachcombers — look out for hermit crabs among the colourful shells and corals (Chris Miller)

4 A weaving demonstration in Nissam (page 113) (Chris Miller)

the fauna of the Western Indian Ocean and the Red Sea. Over 250 species of reef-building coral have been recorded, with at least 730 species of fish. Even if snorkelling is impracticable because of poor weather, the beaches here are richly rewarding for their debris of dead coral, shells and the remnants of other marine creatures (in 2020 there were the dried-out bodies of literally thousands of puffer fish, washed ashore in a cyclone). Remember, take only photos. It is illegal to take any shells etc away with you, and you will be thoroughly searched at the airport to make sure you comply.

Some sandy beaches in the north are nesting sites for loggerhead turtles which come ashore to lay their eggs between May and September. Sadly there are recent reports that these are being caught and eaten, despite being a protected species.

DIHAMRI MARINE NATURE SANCTUARY Within Socotra's Conservation Zoning Plan (page 163) Dihamri is classed as a Marine Nature Sanctuary, as is Rosh (see below), which theoretically affords them the highest level of protection. Commonly referred to by locals as Dihamri Marine Protected Area, or just Dihamri, this sanctuary is home to one of the richest coral reefs in the archipelago so, if the weather is calm, this is a great place for snorkelling. Chris writes, 'Excellent snorkelling opportunities straight off the beach. In December there was 15–20m visibility, lots of corals and colourful fish, plus a chance of seeing turtles, reef sharks, nurse sharks, huge leopard moray eels, octopus, crayfish, various rays, barracuda, scorpion fish, as well as dolphins further out to sea.' At the eastern end of the beach are an extraordinary pair of orange-coloured pyramid-shaped rocks that make for a favoured vantage point at sunset, as well as for guides in search of a mobile signal. There is a popular campsite at the western end, with sun shelters plus good bathroom and kitchen facilities that were built with support from the United Nations Development Programme (UNDP). Snorkelling equipment is available for hire, and the best snorkelling is along the shoreline between the camp and the pyramid rocks, though if the conditions and visibility are good you might also want to try heading a bit further into deeper water where you'll have a better chance of seeing some of the larger aquatic wildlife. If it's too rough to snorkel, Dihamri beach is richly rewarding with its carpets of coral fragments and shells. Close to the camp is a diving centre (page 55) which acts as a base for diving on the whole island, as well as for ongoing marine research in the area – though be wary of strong currents.

ROSH MARINE NATURE SANCTUARY The protected area's reef is about 1km offshore, necessitating a boat ride if you want to dive (page 55) or snorkel there. There is, however, also excellent coral and fish to be seen right off the beach, with easy access for snorkelling from the bay at the southeastern end of the beach near the cliffs. The beach itself is fabulous for shells and coral fragments; you can spend an hour just happily poking around and photographing (no collecting, remember). There is an attractive new campsite with facilities being built a short walk from the beach with help from the UNDP. It was being worked on very actively when Chris and Miranda visited there in March 2024 and should be open by the time this book is published.

SOCOTRA FOLK MUSEUM

At Riqeleh village, on the right of the coast road as you drive eastward from Qaria, this bright little museum is easy to spot. In just one room, there's a collection of traditional household items, including various implements, bags, pots, jars, grinders, a child's hanging cradle, a loom, old photos, an old log canoe, a fire-making set (which the attendant may be happy to demonstrate) and much more.

Outside there's a small display of medicinal plants. Nicole tells that on her last visit her driver demonstrated how to use several of the items, including the cradle (for this he even mimicked the baby crying!) and the traditional wrap worn by both men and women. The museum officially opened in 2008 but its founder Ahmad Saad Khamis Tahki considered that it dated from 1999, which is when he first began collecting items. There's a good account in *Islands of Heritage* by Nathalie Peutz (page 158). There is (reasonably) a small entrance fee but nowhere else on Socotra gives you such a picture of the past so it's worth a look; an explanatory list of the museum contents (in English and Socotri) is available. Ask your guide to check beforehand that it will be open. If you want your own fire-making set, look for them in the Honey Center in Hadiboh (page 68).

HOQ CAVE

Hoq Cave is of immense importance from an archaeological perspective and tells us much about the ancient inhabitants of Socotra, but tourists are, wisely, not allowed to see the delicate pictograms in its inner chambers (see below for further details) which include one of a ship dating from around the 2nd century AD. For us it is the wonderful stalactites and stalagmites which make this cave so special, uncommercialised and unenhanced, as well as the walk up with its wealth of plants and wildlife.

The hike up to Hoq takes some effort, with an altitude gain of 360m, but should not be missed if you can manage it. It's around 9km for the round trip (including the walk inside the cave) and took us 5 hours in total from the starting point at Terbak village (2 hours up to the mouth of the cave). Younger, fitter people are faster (Chris did it in an hour and measured it as 2km to the cave mouth).

If you have done the walk up to Homhil, this is very similar, starting with a flattish section and getting progressively steeper. Wear good shoes or hiking boots; the loose gravel is slippery and there are some steep rocks to clamber up (and down). Walking over the wet mud in the cave is like negotiating a sloping ice rink. A hiking pole is very helpful, and a head-torch is much preferable to a hand-held torch because it leaves both hands free.

| HOQ CAVE | *Julian Jansen van Rensburg* |

This cave is one of Socotra's most important archaeological sites and traces the arrival of visitors to Socotra from the 1st century BC up until the 6th century AD. Throughout Hoq Cave archaeologists have recorded a series of inscriptions, pictograms and artefacts, and at the entrance are examples of some of the later medieval structures and water basins. The cave is believed to have been a religious sanctuary for mariners visiting the island who wrote their names in Indian Brahmi, South Arabian, Palymrene and Bactrian scripts. These scripts were drawn using mud or charcoal and as such are extremely fragile and sensitive to the change that even a single visitor can bring. To prevent these scripts from being damaged and to preserve them for future generations we ask that all visitors to Hoq Cave do not progress beyond the marked area and refrain from smoking in the cave.

Further information on Hoq Cave and other rock art on Socotra can be found at: W soqotraculturalheritage.org/rock-art; also see *Further information* (page 160).

Although the ascent can be done in an hour, the incline, plants, creatures, and views entice one to go slowly – there is so much to examine, photograph and marvel at. The bottle trees are particularly gorgeous; some are almost golden in colour, some very tubby and clinging to rocks – all demanding to have their picture taken. Sadly, though, quite a few have been defaced by graffiti.

One tree you'll see plenty of is *Jatropha unicostata*, a smallish tree in the euphorbia family, with elongated leaves and little, greenish flowers. Although the wood and fruit of this tree are of no use to the locals the sap has many medicinal uses. It makes a very effective 'sticking plaster' for cuts, sealing them against flies and infection. It is also used to heal the wound of a circumcision.

You will also pass several of the largest tree species on the island, the non-endemic *Sterculia africana*. This is a widespread species but the one on Socotra may be an endemic variety. It has a large, beautiful and almost mauve trunk and the leaves are crowded at the end of its branches. The trunk often plays host to the little massed *Achatinelloides* snails (page 14) so look out for these. Leaves of this tree are often fed to goats and cattle, which grow fat on them, and the ripe seeds are sometimes ground up to use as flour. Fruit can be mashed up to use as a shampoo to get rid of nits and head lice.

As well as the plants there is plenty of wildlife to look out for. You'll easily spot the Socotran rock gecko and skink, and may get lucky with other species of reptile. There are grasshoppers aplenty and butterflies. Birds flit around tantalisingly in the treetops but you may spot a Socotran sparrow and certainly starlings, though these are most likely to be Somali starlings (page 21).

You will spot the large cave entrance from about two-thirds of the way up, and as soon as you enter you can see how special this place is. A short way inside, and still lit by natural light, is a huge and very phallic stalagmite (see photo, page 102). It reminds our guide of a mosque minaret. Um... maybe. As you go deeper there are more extraordinary stalagmites and stalactites, patterned and shaped by millions of years of lime-rich water.

The cave is around 3km deep, but you will probably find the permitted 1km far enough. The slipperiness underfoot requires quite a bit of attention. At one point the guide will suggest you all turn off your torches and stand quietly to appreciate the total blackness.

THE EASTERN TIP: ARHER

The sandy area in front of the huge dunes on the north coast is perhaps Socotra's most iconic campsite. It's the ideal location for visiting the northeast attractions as well as the extreme eastern ones and worth staying for two nights if your itinerary allows it. It does, however, suffer from its popularity both with foreign tourists and with mainland Yemeni who like to come over here to picnic on Fridays. If you can avoid this day, do. Because it's so popular it is, sadly, rubbish-strewn. We did a clean-up and you might like to do the same. It is possible to camp either side of the road and the whole way along the dunes, though there is only one public bathroom facility near the western side of the camping areas, which isn't anywhere near enough given the size of the area and its popularity. There is also a private campsite with facilities about a kilometre further southeast of the dunes and 100m inland from the beach, run by the Welcome to Socotra tour company.

It's the **sand dunes** that are the standout feature here and they are extraordinary: sugar-white sand piled up to 400m against the granite cliff, and the other side of the road from the beach. It doesn't quite make sense. The energetic will climb

Julian Glover

For me no single place on the island captures the strange magic of Socotra. My mind races through a jumble of images.

Abandoned army tanks rusting above a pristine sea. Ancient dragon's blood trees lining hills in the sunset like titanic fungi. The spirit-lowering, plastic-littered, concrete-crushed squalor of Hadiboh and the kindness and welcome from the people who live there and throughout the island. The battle of flags: South Yemeni, Emirati, Saudi. The absolute absence of any sign that this place was, until 1967, under British protection – not a rusting EIIR postbox or dented District Commissioner's office in sight.

Swimming in rivers of a size that makes no sense on an island often so hot and dry. A cave, kilometres deep, and a mountain summit I wished I had climbed, 1,503m up in the mists in what must be the finest part of the island. Wild driving in cars with no number plates, wishing you were moving instead with the gentle pad of camels' feet. The bursts of greenery shooting out wherever feral goats cannot get to them – and dreaming at night of obliterating those goats, rifle shot by rifle shot until every one is dead and the island's flora has a future, which it does not now.

The thought that Somalia is not so far over the horizon and with it the joys of Africa, and that Socotra is neither wholly Arabian nor African but a creation which draws on both.

But if I had to pick one image of all, it is this: the vast dunes piled against volcanic cliffs by the sea at Arher. Fresh water pours out at their base, but the climb up is dry, trackless and thigh-burningly hard. In bare feet, in white sand, is it better to charge up direct, and rest every 100 paces? Or track sideways along the ridge? Or cut a diagonal as you climb up the slope? What stands out is a distant campsite below, the sea stretching away, the sand and black rock in front and, when you get to the top, a blade of sand that is somehow strong enough to hold you up even as it slides down beneath your feet. Then the charge down, leaping, almost flying, forgetting the peril of a twisted ankle in this lonely place.

---

them – and some, like Chris, will do it pre-dawn for the view, but then he's a photographer. 'We left our tents at around 3am to watch (and of course photograph!) the bioluminescence (page 102) and skies until around 4:45am. We then made a mad dash to get to the top of the dune for sunrise. We underestimated how hard that climb would be, and also made the mistake of going directly up the soft front rather than taking the firmer and less steep ridge up the western side. It took us around 35 minutes of hard slog and we were a sweaty mess by the time we got up there. Definitely worth it though!'

I'm not a pre-dawn riser so sat happily on a chair, sipping sweetened tea and watching members of our group crawling on hands and knees towards the top (page 104). There are three dunes; the highest central one, above the campsite, is the most often climbed, but the others often have their specks of humanity labouring towards the top too.

As if the dunes weren't enough to marvel at, this is the best place to see the phenomenon of **bioluminescence**, an extraordinary trick of nature where animals (and fungi) emit a blue light. No-one really knows why. It is commonly a marine feature, particularly with zooplankton, animals that consist largely of water such as jellyfish. Chris reports: 'While snorkelling at Dihamri a few days later we saw quite a lot of tiny disc-like organisms drifting in the water that glowed a beautiful pale blue. If you reached out to try and touch them, their light would go out and they'd instantly disappear. I imagine they were the same thing that causes the bioluminescence in the surf at Arher.'

Several freshwater streams run – somewhat miraculously – from the dunes (actually from the cliffs behind them) and attract wading birds to the sandy beach. Bring your binoculars and look out for Kentish plover, Heuglin's gull, sooty gulls and great crested terns. Noddys are also sometimes present. You might also see brown boobies offshore and, while looking out to sea, keep watch for dolphins and even killer whales. One of the fresh streams runs through the edge of the campsite, so you can paddle in fresh, warm water or even secrete yourself behind the bushes and have a wash; but look out for the soft patches of sand further up, where there's a risk of sinking in.

Finally, the small sandy beaches that stretch out along this coast are some of the best places anywhere for a swim, or to search out some attractive shells – only to look at and photograph, of course!

RAS ERISSEL VIEWPOINT HIKE For the more energetic among you, there is a less well-known but excellent hike that starts from a parking spot at some abandoned huts a few minutes away from the dunes (⊕ 12°32'31.5"N 54°28'37.8"E), and takes you up on to the ridge that can be seen rising up front of you. The route isn't marked or well trodden, so if your guide isn't sure of the best way up they may want to ask around for a local to guide you. Even at a good pace it will take around an hour to make your way up to the ridge, and you'll gain a hard-earned 300m of altitude in the process, so be sure to wear sturdy shoes and take plenty of water with you. Unlike the hikes up to Homhil and Hoq, the route is rather barren with no bottle trees to marvel at on the way up, plus the ascent is somewhat steeper, especially towards the end. The effort is well worth it though; once at the top you'll be quickly and richly rewarded with remarkable 360° views of the rugged cliffs above the Arher dunes, Ras Erissel off to the east, and the dramatic northern and southern coastlines stretching off into the far distance below.

The ridge-top itself is mercifully flat and extends about a kilometre to the east before gradually narrowing to a photogenic rocky point, beyond which it would be difficult to go much further. You can easily spend an hour or more exploring the whole ridge-top area, soaking up the scenery, relaxing and taking photos, before eventually and reluctantly deciding it's time to head back down the way you came.

RAS ERISSEL

The long spit of land which makes up the extreme eastern nose of Socotra is a place of wild seas and beaches littered with shells, coral and the remains of other marine life including the enormous bones of a whale. It is also the place where two oceans meet: the Arabian Sea to the north and the Indian Ocean to the south. Unless they're out at sea, some colourful local fishing boats are generally pulled up on a sheltered stretch of the southern shore, where there are also a few stone storage sheds (⊕ 12°32'21.0"N 54°30'59.9"E). Ask here if you want to hire a boat to take you to the start of the walk to Killisan (page 97). Scuba diving (page 55) is also possible here with a range of dive sites on offer; at most of them you'll be able to explore an unfortunate shipwreck or two.

The fringe of the whole spit is a series of sand and coral beaches separated by rocky promontories. The shells here were the best anywhere (yes, that's right, no

This peninsula with its dunes and sandy beaches is so peaceful in good weather, but in June 1897 the SS *Aden*, a P&O vessel carrying cargo and 34 passengers, ran into desperate trouble barely a mile offshore. Heading home from the Far East to England via Suez, it had left Colombo on 3 June and been hit by the full force of a monsoon storm the next day. In appalling conditions it pitched and rolled its way north up the Indian Ocean until, at 03.00 on 9 June, it crashed on to a reef about a mile north of Arher. The lights failed and in pitch darkness the British passengers (who included 12 children described as 'of tender years' and two aged 11 to 13, plus three Chinese nurses caring for them), grabbed some semblance of clothing and struggled up on deck. Three lifeboats and a dinghy had been smashed on impact and two more were swept away when launched. Eight women and nine infants were piled into the final lifeboat and it made off, but did not survive. Some officers and crew members had already died in the efforts of launching the boats, while the sea continued to crash over the broken ship and those still on board. Pounded by waves and dashed violently from side to side of the deck, the 17 remaining passengers gradually dwindled to nine as more (including three infants and the ship's captain) were swept away one by one. Then the extraordinary tale of survival began.

The ship, although badly damaged, held fast on the reef. The whole of the wooden structure in front was gone, the bridge and chart room, captain's table, and the roofing and sides of the companionway, leaving the stairway to the saloon open to the seas. The exhausted and injured survivors dragged themselves into a small intact cabin for the night, cold, wet, hungry, frightened, in pain and grieving for the loved ones they had lost. Next day, with heavy seas still sweeping over the ship, a risky sortie to search for food yielded '10lbs of Barcelona nuts, about half a tin (5lbs) of small biscuits, one or two tins of fruit…soda water, tonic…two or three bottles of whisky…' And there they stayed for 17 days, three men, four women and two young children plus two of the ship's engineers, gradually venturing further around the broken ship as the storm abated to find more food. The 33 surviving members of the ship's crew, described as Portuguese and Lascar, were holed up in different areas and hard to access safely. On 13 June a ship passed by but didn't stop, believing no-one could have survived on such a wreck, and reported it later in Suez. On 17 June another passed, heading towards Socotra, but missed or ignored their signals. On 22 June, Queen Victoria's Jubilee Day, the battered little group toasted Her Majesty in whisky and water. A further foray for food produced two large uncooked hams, which they tucked into joyfully. Finally on 26 June the Royal Indian Marine steamship *Mayo* arrived and took them aboard; it had been dispatched to check the area after the wreck was reported in Suez.

The death toll had reached 78. Installing warning lights on Socotra was discussed, but nothing was done. *The Times* (of London) dated 17 July 1897 carries a fuller account, by one of the survivors. No trace of the wreck remains today, whether above or below the waves, but give its crew and passengers a thought as you slide happily down Arher's sand dune or bask on its beaches!

collecting!) and on our visit we found ourselves walking on the prickly dried-up bodies of thousands of puffer fish which had been washed there by a winter storm. They tend to swim quite close to the surface of the water so, when waves crash ashore, unfortunately so do they. The spines of these little skeletons break up into countless little caltrop-shaped weapons, strong enough to get quite firmly stuck in rubber flip-flops and, together with the broken coral, mean that you shouldn't walk on these beaches barefoot.

To the east is one of the north shore's '**crab cities**', another extraordinary phenomenon, where ghost crabs (page 18) have excavated high-rise mounds, and sit inside the entrance to their holes trying to find a mate, as well as keeping wary watch on visitors with their comical stalk eyes.

There is no designated campsite here, or any facilities at all for that matter, but you can camp on some of the little beaches at the very eastern tip of Socotra where you'll likely have the whole place to yourselves. The swimming is wonderful, as are the sunrises and sunsets, and there's a chance of seeing dolphins passing by just offshore.

Alan Forrest writes: 'The Ras Erissel region has excellent and particularly diverse examples of the island's coastal vegetation. These include a range of endemic species, including one of the few locations for the attractive pale-yellow-flowered *Lachnocapsa spathulata*.'

Nissam, the scattered village on the tip, inland of the road amid low dunes, is friendly and unfazed by visitors. As you approach the village you may see children on the side of the road holding out rugs and other locally woven products for sale. One interesting item they may offer are are big woollen loops, which you can put around your back and shins to sit comfortably cross legged without other support – who needs chairs! Chris and Miranda were invited in to one of the houses to watch the women weave: 'We learned that it's a very labour-intensive process, with the wool having to be shorn, spun, then dyed with turmeric by the women, all by hand (page 69). The loom is a simple rig of strings and wooden sticks, strung between the ceiling and floor of the house. For each lengthwise (warp) thread, the weaver throws the ball of wool from their end of the loom to an assistant at the other, who loops it then throws it back again. Our guide Ruslan proved quite proficient when asked to help out in this role'.

When passing through this area on their previous trip they found a small pharmacy nearby and, as their Socotra trip was nearing its end, gave it their left-over first-aid equipment. That's something we can all remember: there's little point in cluttering our homeward-bound suitcases with things we don't really need, when they can be put to better use on the island.

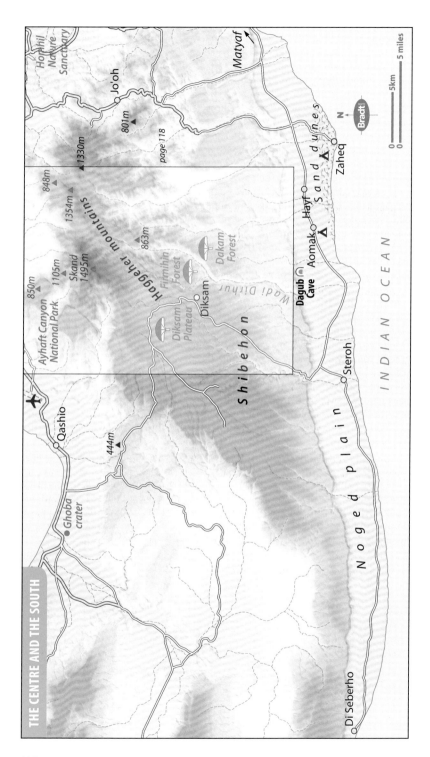

THE CENTRE AND THE SOUTH

Hoq Hill Nature Sanctuary

Jo'oh

801m ▲

▲1330m

Matyaf

page 118

Sand dunes

Zaheq

Aomak Hayf

Bradt

N

0   5km
0   5 miles

848m ▲

1354m ▲

Haggeher mountains

863m ▲

Firmihin Forest

Dakam Forest

850m ▲

1105m ▲
Skand
1495m ▲

Ayhaft Canyon National Park

Diksam Plateau

Diksam

Dagub Cave

Wadi Dirhur

Shibehon

Qashio

444m ▲

Ghoba crater

Steroh

INDIAN OCEAN

Noged plain

Di Seberho

5

The Centre and the South

The beauty of the view presented by the Haghier slopes and summits, it would be difficult to exaggerate. . . . [The party was] soothed to sleep by the 'song of the setting sun' [ie the Socotra scops owl].

Henry Ogg Forbes, 1898, on the British and
Liverpool Museums Expedition to Socotra

Tucked away in the heart of Socotra you will find the island's most dramatic mountain scenery, its highest points (around 1,500m) and its densest concentration of dragon's blood trees, keeping watch over the hills like squads of military mushrooms. You will also encounter probably the biggest contrast of your trip, as you drive south from the jagged peaks and wind-shaped plateaux of the centre – the 'crown' of the trilby hat described on page xii! – to the dry flat fringe of the southern coast with its giant sand dunes, date palms and silvery beaches.

THE HIGHLANDS

In this area of lonely beauty a canyon (one of several) carves the terrain into two equally fascinating landscapes. Here you have the best chance of seeing some of Socotra's endemic species: if you're lucky you will find the Socotran chameleon (page 19) and even the magnificent blue baboon tarantula spider (page 16), as well as other easier-to-spot invertebrates such as dragonflies and butterflies. And you can tick off several endemic bird species. Richard Porter writes: 'The highland areas of Socotra are probably the richest for the island's special birds and a keen birdwatcher could expect to see nine of the twelve endemic species. Look out for the Socotra sunbird, Socotra white-eye (recently elevated to endemic status), Socotra starling and Socotra golden-winged grosbeak. More difficult to spot will be the Socotra warbler and you will have to be very lucky to spy the rare and rather secretive Socotra bunting. Overhead the occasional Socotra buzzard will be soaring and at night you are sure to hear the monotonous song of the Socotra scops owl.'

For trekkers it is the route into the Haggeher mountains, and other seldom-visited canyons (wadis) such as the beautiful Wadi Zeyrig, where Socotra's unique damselflies (page 16) can be seen. Socotra at its best.

WADI DIRHUR

Also known as the Diksam Gorge, this place seems as though a giant has pulled a huge slab of soft limestone apart like a hunk of cheese, and then poured cool, clear water down the crack specifically for the delight of visitors.

Mostly visitors will be looking down at the canyon, all 700m of it, and using its drama as a backdrop to their photos, but a dirt road crosses it at one point, where there are sun shelters for day visitors on the eastern bank, as well as a small camping area with toilet facilities for overnight stays. There are no showers here, but if you follow the wadi downstream, within a few minutes' walk are some gorgeous crab-filled paddling and swimming pools (see Matthew Parris's description, opposite).

DIKSAM PLATEAU AND VILLAGE

The limestone plateau, on the western side of the gorge, has some photogenic dragon's blood trees and bottle trees. Being within an easy walk of the popular Diksam campsite, it also provides keen photographers with the chance of getting those sunrise and sunset shots that they've been yearning for. Chris, who will sacrifice all his sleep for the right photos says: 'There are several dragon's blood trees near the campsite that make for good sunset photos, but for the best sunrise views you can follow the canyon south where you will find some very photogenic dragons near the edge of the gorge. You can also continue further up towards the village at Diksam, where you'll pass some very large and isolated dragons that are great for night shots of trees against a starry sky.'

Diksam Plateau is the starting point for a trek into the Haggeher mountains to Skand (page 132), a 16km round trip, with a 600m gain and loss in altitude, which takes a fit person about 8 hours. There are also shorter, more level hikes along the edge of the canyon where you can see the Bedouin houses built into ledges where the plateau meets the canyon. The difficult-to-see Socotra bunting can also be found not too far from here, though you will likely need a good local guide to help find them. Chris and Miranda managed to see several on their second trip to Socotra with the help of their guide Ruslan from I Love Socotra, who knew a few good locations where they are more easily seen.

There is also a Bedouin school in the main village, and with prior arrangement with your tour operator it is usually possible to visit this, meet the children, and pass on educational materials; see also page 70.

CAMPING AT DIKSAM There is one main campsite at Diksam, located right on the edge of Wadi Dirhur, with spectacular views up and down the gorge as well as across to Firmihin Forest, especially at sunrise. It has toilet and shower facilities, and as of March 2024 construction was well under way to expand the campsite significantly to help accommodate the increasing numbers of visitors. It is a very popular location due to the wonderful scenery and its convenience as an overnight stop-off when travelling between the north and south of the island. Despite the crowds, it makes a good base for exploration, and was the only place we managed a **night walk** and were able to pick out the eyeshine of wolf spiders (page 16). Up until recently it was possible to stay in Diksam village itself, at a camp called the Homestay Campsite run by a local family. As of the time of writing this is currently closed to visitors, however there is a possibility it will reopen again soon.

FIRMIHIN FOREST

On the eastern side of Wadi Dirhur is the largest area of easily accessible dragon's blood trees on Socotra, and a must for all visitors. You can take long or short walks to see the trees, not just dragon's blood but desert roses and other bottle trees including cucumber trees, and accompanying wildlife. Most likely you will be given a demonstration of tapping the dragon's blood trunks for resin, and the chance to buy it in its solidified form – and to wonder, when you get home, what to do with it. There is a large and popular camping area in the forest, however at the time of writing it had no bathroom facilities and as a result the surrounding forest was rather unpleasantly dotted with toilet paper, which was a real shame to see.

The camping area is a short walk from the local village, where you can find Mr Suliman's wonderful small nursery of young dragon's blood trees, frankincense and various other native species, grown using skills passed on from the Keybani family's nursery at Ras Ayre (page 121). Once the dragons get big enough they are relocated to the fenced-off area you'll see right next to the camp. The nursery is struggling for funding, so any donations you are able to make will be extremely gratefully received. After visiting the nursery, Mr Suliman's friendly wife Fatima will likely invite you to sit for tea. She also has a selection of local pottery, frankincense and *dareb* (tooth cleaning twigs from the kaleh tree) for sale at fair prices.

HADIBOH TO DIKSAM CAMEL TREK   *Chris Miller*

While Miranda and I were researching our trip to Socotra, we decided to start with a trek with camels from Hadiboh to Diksam via the Haggeher mountains. The five-day itinerary was to take us from the base of the mountains up to one of their highest peaks, down again to Wadi Sha'ab and Wadi Da'asqalah, then up and over to Wadi Dirhur via Roukab Plateau and Firmihin Forest. From there we would continue up on to Diksam Plateau, finishing with a round trip from Diksam up to Skand and back. Over the five days we ended up covering 52km, ascending 3,100m and descending 2,500m. Here is my diary of those five days.

A FRESHWATER SWIM   *Matthew Parris*

Your experience of Socotra will be stamped by the ocean. Wherever you are the ocean feels near. You are looking at the ocean, or your back is to the ocean, or from the nearest peak or pass you can see the ocean spread at your feet. The noise you'll remember is of the wind and the waves, great rollers crashing onto the shore. All islands have interiors but Socotra hides hers, and always points you back to the sea.

For me there was one exception, one peek into Socotra's hidden heart. Right through the middle of the island snakes a remarkable canyon. Between sheer rock walls and surely a thousand feet below the plateau, winds a clear, clean river. Washing over stones, lingering in cool, deep, turquoise pools, fringed with palms and pink-flowering bottle trees, the Wadi Dirhur eddies through what – when you're down there – feels almost to be a tunnel, tight with greenery, beneath the dry plateau which it cleaves like a cheese-knife. The precipitous track down one side and up the other is a little miracle in road-making; and as you bounce down between great desert boulders, the heat growing and the colours all reds and browns, the allure of what could lie at the bottom grows.

You arrive finally in what feels like an oasis. There are pools. You can swim, dangle your feet in the water, explore as far as you like, and watch the endemic pink crabs scuttle away. Perhaps in a temperate European setting this secret gorge would not feel so special; but here, hidden from the ocean and defying the aridity all around, the Wadi Dirhur feels like a miracle.

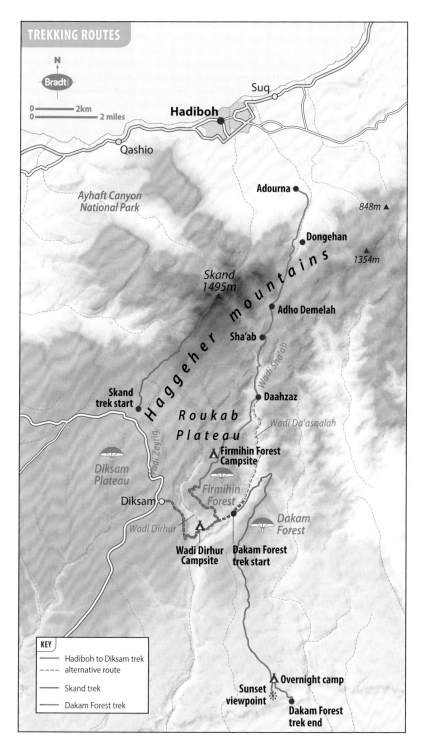

Julian Jansen van Rensburg and the Soqotra Heritage Project team

The tour companies in Hadiboh include camel trekking in their programmes, or will do so if asked. They offer various itineraries, taking you along the mountain tracks followed by earlier explorers and beyond, depending on your available time and level of fitness.

When the camel first arrived on Socotra and where it came from is not clear, although at the rock art site of Eriosh you can see several images of camels. Sadly, this site and the images cannot be dated accurately, although it is known that camels were introduced rather than native to the island. The earliest known account of them on Socotra was by Lieutenant James Wellsted who, in 1834, recommended that all travellers on Socotra with occasion to journey should do so on camels. However, he later explains how, during a particularly steep crossing, they almost lost a camel as it slipped off the path:

> …and slid down to some distance, until his progress to destruction was stopped by his inserting the joint of his hinder legs into a hollow, whence he contrived cautiously to regain his footing: a few yards farther, and he would have rolled over the precipice, and been dashed to pieces on the rocks below.

The Arab owners of these camels were said to have come from mainland Yemen, bringing with them an archaic South Arabian type of camel saddle found in Somalia and now Socotra. Recent studies also suggest that camels may well have been on trading vessels to northern Africa and possibly Socotra from the early first millennium BC, and increasingly from the Ptolemaic period (305–30 BC). They were still used frequently by explorers on the island until at least the 1990s as there were few cars and even fewer roads.

DAY 1: HADIBOH TO HAGGEHER MOUNTAINS *(8km; 6hrs inc stops)*

We began with a short drive to the small village of Adourna on the outskirts of Hadiboh where Miranda, Ruslan (our guide throughout our visit) and I were met by our local Bedouin guides Eisa and Abdullah. They were waiting with two of their camels which were loaded up with cooking equipment, food, tents and other supplies. That included bottled water, but a water filter saved us using most of those as there were plenty of clean wadis to fill up from along the way, and the island has a problem with plastic waste.

We followed a red dirt road that had been badly damaged by recent storms and was no longer usable by vehicles. It wound up into the Haggeher mountains and, as we gained altitude, the views back down to the northern coast kept getting better and our surroundings became a lush green. After about 1.5km we could see across a small valley to a place called Dongehan, where there are natural rock pools that are often visited by the locals from Hadiboh for picnics and swimming.

About 2 hours into our trek we stopped under a Namaqua fig tree (*Ficus fusta*), popular with many bird species, and unloaded the camels for lunch, after which we saw our first dragon's blood trees, some right alongside the road. After an hour we arrived at the Haggeher mountain ridge, in among the clouds and over 900m higher than our starting point that morning. The terrain was flattened and mostly pasture, and we saw mountain crabs in the puddles and grasses here. The scenery was truly jaw dropping, with some of the most rugged mountain peaks anywhere, made more dramatic by the rapidly shifting clouds and occasional bursts of sun.

About 20 minutes down from the ridge was Adho Demelah, a Bedouin settlement of three small stone houses, one of which would be our refuge for the next two nights. We were met here by the owner Ali, who would join us as an additional guide for the next couple of days. This place is almost certainly Adho Dimellus, the campsite of the British and Liverpool museums expedition in 1898, described by Forbes as 'The roof of Sokotra' and shown in the photo on page 34.

DAY 2: HAGGEHER MOUNTAINS
Had the weather been fine, our plan for the next day had been to make the 4–5-hour return trek further up the the Haggeher mountains, to the highest peak of the region at around 1,500m. From here there are plenty of possibilities for further hikes, even as far as Skand, but we have no information on them. As it was, the wind, rain and cloud ensured that we spent the day relaxing, drinking tea around a fire, sharing stories, watching and photographing the local birdlife and dramatic changes of weather. Keep an eye out for the pale crag martins that are resident in the area.

DAY 3: ADHO DEMELAH TO DAAHZAZ (8km; 5hrs inc stops)
The following morning we set out for the small settlement of Daahzaz in the valley below. Our camels had been taken part of the way the day before, in anticipation of the wadi level rising from the rains – a wise decision: by the time we arrived at the crossing the water was running swiftly and thigh deep. We made it across, reloaded the camels and continued along a flat path at the bottom of the valley, criss-crossing the wadi a few more times, but in shallower water. Even so, we found shoes (or sandals) that drained quickly much more practical here than waterproof hiking boots as we got pretty wet each time.

After following the wadi for half an hour or so a short uphill hike took us to a ridge top called Dahamder, with a good view south down into the valley with the river flowing through beautiful pink boulders. From here it was an easy descent through rocky meadows, with views of dry wadis and more pink boulders with the added treat of a wonderful Socotran chameleon crossing our path.

After about half an hour we arrived at Sha'ab where there was a small Bedouin plantation. We were treated to some fresh bananas and guavas, before continuing for another hour down the valley, walking on the pink boulders alongside the wadi, crossing it twice before reaching the settlement of Daahzaz. We overnighted in a Bedouin house here, conveniently close to Wadi Da'asqalah for a refreshing dip and wash. Our guides put up the tent inside the house to give us some privacy, as we were all sleeping in the same building. On a night walk we found many chameleons as well as various other reptiles, insects, spiders and birds sleeping in the trees.

DAY 4: DAAHZAZ TO DIKSAM VIA WADI DIRHUR AND FIRMIHIN FOREST (16km; 9hrs inc stops)
This morning we bid farewell to our camels, which would be taking a more direct route to Wadi Dirhur. We followed Wadi Da'asqalah for about 20 minutes, crossing it a few times before reaching the beginning of our ascent up to a ridgeline 150m above. Initially the face looked too steep to climb, but after a short rocky scramble there was something of a path that zigzagged its way upwards. Whether this route was more suited to goats rather than humans is open to debate, however!

Throughout the 40-minute climb the views back the way we'd come were spectacular, and once we reached the ridge we were rewarded with wonderful views of Wadi Da'asqalah to the south. Another hour was spent walking uphill along the ridge, but with the interest of many different plants including aloe, a large variety of wildflowers and the occasional bottle tree.

By the time we'd reached the top we'd gained an additional 200m. The terrain flattened out and the scrub gave way to rocky grassland. This was Roukab Plateau, and as we walked across it we passed close by a small Bedouin community where sheep and goats were being farmed. Close to this settlement is the Firmihin Forest campsite (page 117), and the first of many dragon's blood trees. This was the start of Firmihin Forest with dragon's blood trees all around us and as far as the eye could see. We followed a rough road through the trees for a little over 2 hours, flat initially then gently descending 450m to Wadi Dirhur, where we met up again with our camels. While waiting for lunch we walked about 300m downstream to some natural swimming pools.

A NURSERY OF BABY DRAGONS   *Dr Kay Van Damme*

On your way south from Diksam, ask your driver to take you to the small village called Ras Ayre in the Shibehon area. It holds a unique treasure: the **world's first reforestation area of dragon's blood trees**. Socotra's species of dragon's blood tree, *Dracaena cinnabari*, is already unique; but even in places such as the Canary Islands, where other species of dragon's blood trees occur, there is no similar undertaking. The head of the village, Mohammed Salem Abdullah Masood Keybani, first established a dragon's blood tree nursery (altogether 715 three- to five-year-old *Dracaena cinnabari* seedlings) there in 2006, receiving financial and technical support from a Czech team of foresters from Mendel University. The Keybani family's evident passion and care for these unique trees has inspired and sparked the interest of the children and grandchildren of the village elders, and this is important, because Socotra's dragon's blood trees need the continued care and involvement of local people if the species is to survive. Scientists have calculated that it could take over a century for a tree to carry its first fruits, so their conservation requires really long-term vision and engagement, particularly because recent models by Czech researchers show that in five centuries from now, *without* human intervention and without taking into account global warming, this endangered tree would be driven to extinction. At present, its natural regeneration is limited by overgrazing (goats), drought and cyclone damage. The majority of the trees we see in the landscape are over-mature, and many were destroyed by the 2015 and 2018 cyclones. The nursery is only a first step; what makes the Keybani enterprise unique is that the growing trees are planted directly into the wild, at first protected by a fence which, once they are mature enough to escape browsing pressure, can be removed. This opens up a whole new area of study and development.

The family have built a shelter for visitors where you can pause, picnic and enjoy the view over the young *Dracaena* trees in their nursery. Notice also that there is no rubbish in this village – the family have their own effective system of collection. There is even an excellent phone signal, better than in most areas of Hadiboh. Don't expect huge trees in the nursery, however. Dragons have no sense of urgency! Even after 20 years, these plants look like a spiky rosette on the ground, and take a few centuries to develop the large umbrella shape that is such a typical and welcoming sight on the island.

5

1 & 2 Wadi Dirhur, a gash 700m deep, dividing Diksam Plateau and Firmihin Forest (page 115) (Chris Miller)

3   Diksam village (page 116) (Chris Miller)

4–7 One dragon's blood tree is spectacular, but a forest of them at Firmihin is extraordinary. Guides will demonstrate how the 'blood' (resin) is tapped from the trees. Crystallised pieces, occasionally combined into large lumps, are sold to tourists by local boys. Older trees show the scars of blood letting (page 116).

4 & 6 Nicole Smoot, 5 Soqotra Heritage Project, 7 Hilary Bradt

Diksam Plateau is a photographer's delight at any time of day, but particularly at sunrise and sunset (page 116)

1, 2 & 4 Chris Miller, *3* Lukas Bischoff/S

4

1 & 2　Chris Miller had time to do a camel trek high into the Haggeher Mountains during his first two-week-long visit to the island. These photos illustrate his five-day route from near Hadiboh to Diksam. The route into the mountains begins with a red, dusty road (page 117)

3 & 4　Strong winds and rains forced Chris and Miranda to spend two nights in a Bedouin settlement at Adho Demelah: an opportunity to take some atmospheric photos (page 120)

5 Crossing a wadi near Sha'ab (page 120)

6 Views down into Wadi Da'asqalah (page 120)

1–6 Chris Miller

1 & 2 **Dakam Forest trek** (page 132) (Chris Miller)

3

3 The vast Zaheq dunes (page 134) (Chris Miller)

4 Star gazing at Zaheq (Chris Miller)

4

1 A local woman, near Aomak (page 134) (Chris Miller)

2 Looking out from inside Dagub Cave (page 134) (Nicole Smoot)

3 & 4 Dunes at Steroh, where the distinctive architecture is a result of Saudi Arabia's support in the town's construction (page 135) (Chris Miller)

From the wadi it was a 5km walk up a steep road to Diksam that took a little over 90 minutes – exhausting in the heat, so we'd recommend that your driver pick you up at the wadi.

DAY 5: DIKSAM TO SKAND *(up to 16km round trip; 8hrs inc stops)*

While we did this trek as an extension to our trek from Hadiboh to Diksam, it's really a standalone route that's done in a single day, without camels, starting and finishing from Diksam.

The start of the trek depends on what condition the roads are in. We had to walk further than normal because of the recent rains, probably adding an hour or more to the journey.

We set off through meadowland, following a path that followed a stream for about 40 minutes. After crossing the stream the path fizzled out and we headed up a large open valley, walking through gentle farmland at first, getting steeper as we approached the ridgeline. Beware of 'killer grass' which had sharp hooks that latched on to shoes, socks and clothing! I was lucky enough to be wearing waterproof hiking shoes and hiking trousers made from a finely woven synthetic material, both of which seemed to be too smooth for the hooks to catch on to. Miranda and our guide were not so fortunate, however, and they had an ongoing battle with this grass, mainly during the lower section of the trek. After crossing this first ridge we followed a path down a short, steep, rocky descent before the next uphill stretch. Before long the valley wall to our left gave way to big open ravines and cliffs, with spectacular views all the way to the north coast. This is a great place to stop for a rest and it would be worth the walk just for this if you don't have the fitness for the rest of the hike. From here it was another 90 minutes up to the top of Skand, quite steep in parts and a lot of scrambling through thick bushes in places. Look out for the rare sight of young dragon's blood trees here. When you arrive at the top, congratulations – you've climbed from around 850m up to 1,500m and you're officially the highest people in all of Socotra! If you're lucky and the skies are clear, from the top of Skand you'll have 360° views including both the north and south coasts.

The descent, back the way we came, was easier and towards the bottom we were welcomed into a farmhouse where we stopped for some much-needed sugary tea and fun conversations with the locals. From there it was about another 40 minutes back to our vehicle – a welcome sight! We had covered 16km in around 8 hours including stops, but because of the condition of the road, we had started further back than usual.

DAKAM FOREST CAMEL TREK *Miranda Lindsay-Fynn*

This two-day trek starts near the south side of Firmihin Forest, and takes you through to the south coast via the rather wonderful yet little-visited Dakam Forest. While we did this as a standalone two-day trek on a separate visit to Socotra from our previous camel trekking described above, it is possible to combine the two. If you do decide to combine them, you could also consider following the alternate route via Wadi Da'asqalah rather than going via Roukab Plateau. This will save you a day, and you can still visit Firmihin Forest by vehicle separately.

DAY 1: DAKAM FOREST *(16km; 8hrs inc stops)*

We drove about an hour from our camp at Firmihin to Wadi Da'arho, where the camels were waiting to be loaded up with the food and equipment we'd need for the next couple of days. We headed off in advance of the camels, initially following alongside the wadi before climbing up a winding rocky road. We saw some empty buildings further up, and Eisa 'The Camel Man' explains that it was a school. No-one lives here anymore though, as there has been so much flood damage to houses in the area since the cyclones started in 2015. After an hour and a half of increasingly steep uphill, we suddenly reached an impressive plateau covered with flowering bottle trees and views back to the Haggeher mountains. We walked past a small settlement where we paused for a short break before continuing on to Dakam Forest: a forest of dragon's blood trees. While it's not as big or as dense with dragons as the more famous Firmihin Forest to the north, we both found it far more picturesque than Firmihin due to its nicely spaced combination of dragons interspersed with flowering bottle trees, along with the rugged mountain backdrop that you don't really see so well at Firmihin. It also helped that we had the entire place to ourselves!

We stopped for tea and lunch in the shade of a large dragon's blood tree. After a long and relaxing break, we continued on the plateau where the forest soon thinned out and turned into dry rocky rolling grassland, criss-crossed with Agars – lines of ancient rocks that were built before the current known history of Socotra. Folklore has it that they were constructed to help direct water movement in the rainy season and also prevent soil erosion, but no one seems to really know for sure. Small villages with houses made of stone blend seamlessly into the hillside. The villages we encountered here were also no longer inhabited; the villagers have moved to the south coast where there are schools. We soon passed a goat farmer heading back home and after a short negotiation with Eisa, he turned around and headed back to get us a whole goat for dinner. Soon after, we arrived alongside an old abandoned well where we would be camping for the night. Sunset was fast approaching, so we quickly decided to head about 1km along a rocky route to a viewpoint with what turned out to be fantastic views of the south coast. We could see the alluvial plains with drainage coming off the mountainside and Zaheq's vast rippling sand dunes stretching out along the Indian Ocean coastline, all bathed in the setting sun.

Returning back down to camp in the fading light, we were invited to have dinner Socotran style with our Bedouin hosts. The goat had been poached, and to start with the ribs, bones and liver were shared, then the broth was passed around, after which the meat was finally served as the main meal.

DAY 2: TOWARDS THE SOUTH COAST *(2km; 1hr)*

We were initially told it would be about 3–4 hours to our destination, so we packed and set off with that in mind. The route started off fairly flat but soon started to descend down a rocky trail winding its way through an area of pretty bottle trees. It was still early, but by the time we had passed through most of this area it was already getting quite hot. I was feeling a bit ill and Chris had a problem with his ankle, so the progress was slower going than we'd have liked. Fortunately our guide Ruslan had a solution. He phoned ahead to our driver Adel, who said he would come up the very rough road to collect us – much to our relief. Once Adel arrived, we unloaded our gear from the camels into the 4x4, bade farewell to Eisa and the camel herders, then drove down to the beach at Aomak to recover over a lazy lunch and relaxing swim.

Even though being picked up earlier than intended made for a rather short second day of trekking, in hindsight this was probably what we should have planned anyway. The rest of the hike down would have been following the same road we drove down, where there was less remarkable scenery than the views up

5

around the campsite, or indeed the marvels of the plateau and Dakam Forest from the previous day.

THE SOUTH COAST

Continuing southward from Diksam and its dragons you arrive in a very different landscape. The island's sparsely populated southern plains are mainly notable for the vast sand dunes shown in numerous photos, and some good opportunities for sea swimming – if it is not too windy – from (predictably) sandy beaches. From Matyaf village at the eastern end (about 25km east of Zaheq on sometimes uncertain roads) you can take a 2-hour trek up to the wonderful freshwater pools of Killisan; page 97.

There is currently no usable through road along the coast from Ras Erissel (page 111), so (unless it has been recently refurbished) to reach the places described here you must either cross the centre of the island from the north or follow the slow and bumpy, but very scenic, Melalahan Road (page 97) from Momi Plateau.

ZAHEQ DUNES   When standing on one of these dunes it's easy to believe that you're in the Sahara Desert, or that Lawrence of Arabia may appear from the shimmering haze. In contrast to Arher (page 109) the dune area is huge, with rippled sand stretching to the horizon. Socotra's camels browse on the *Indigofera pseudointricata* bushes near the dunes so this is the most likely place to see them if you are not doing a camel trek. For birders, Richard Porter adds: 'on the plains and in the dunes look out for black-crowned sparrow-larks, desert wheatears and long-billed pipits; if you are lucky you might spot a cream-coloured courser. The tiny, endemic Socotra cisticola nests in the low scrub – listen out for its repeated "zip-zip" in its undulating song flight.' The flat area near the scrub is littered with the shells of land snails. The beach and sea are a 40-minute walk beyond the dunes so a bit too much effort for most people, who will save their swim for Aomak further to the west. **Hayf** is a similar dune area, smaller but still spectacular, just to the west of Zaheq. Along all of this coastal plain watch out for sand blowing in the air on windy days – it's not good for either eyes or cameras.

AOMAK BEACH   This is a popular campsite with shower and bathroom facilities, and picnic places under a grove of date palms with the sea conveniently close and inviting. However, be wary of the strong currents and powerful waves – this beach has also been popular for wind-surfing and kite-surfing (not available for hire anywhere at the time of writing – you would have to bring your own) because it's almost always windy. Be prepared to be sand-blasted! Perhaps Marco Polo had a point, when he wrote:

> The Sokotrans are enchanters as great as any in the world… They raise winds to bring back such ships as have wronged them till they obtain satisfaction… They can in like manner cause the sea to become calm, and at their will raise tempests, occasion shipwrecks, and produce many other extraordinary effects…
>
> Marco Polo, c1293

DAGUB CAVE   Directly north of Aomak is the turning to Dagub Cave. We have to admit that if there were any popular site that we would omit in a Socotra itinerary it would be this. But maybe we were spoiled by Hoq Cave which ticked all the boxes.

You can drive almost to the cave entrance, which makes it a popular picnic site for the locals. This popularity had resulted – when we were there – in a large amount of rubbish, from either locals or other tourists, so it would be kind to take a bag with you and do a quick clean-up. The cave entrance is huge, giving a spectacular coastal view, and small birds chirp and flitter in the surrounding bushes. There are a few stalactites and stalagmites as you go inside, where there is also a small 'basin' of fresh water. The most interesting feature is probably the bats that roost high up at the back of the cave, mostly on the right as you face inwards. They are lesser mouse-tailed bats, and it's strange to see a bat with a long tail!

STEROH West of Aomak is the fishing village Steroh, nestled on the coast with some very picturesque, pristine white sand dunes nearby that are well worth a bit of a climb. The architecture of Steroh is quite different to the rest of Socotra as the village was rebuilt with Saudi support following typhoon damage. You can see the influence; houses are modern whitewashed square buildings with rooftop water tanks.

It is now possible to wild camp either near the beach or in among the dunes. It's a great place to watch the fishing boats come and go, or explore the dunes at sunset, although at the time of writing there were no facilities.

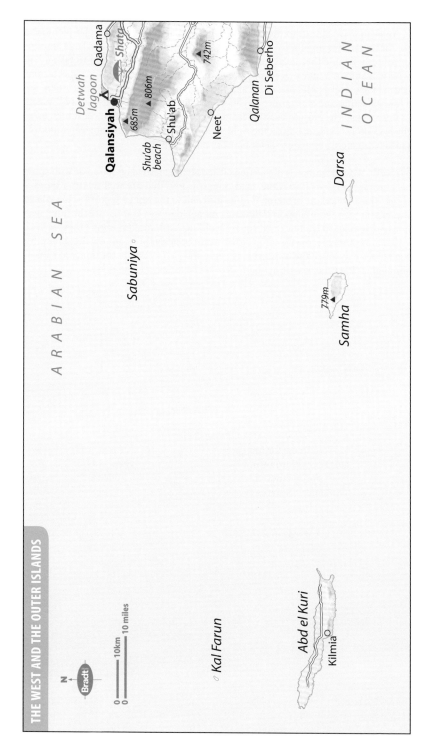

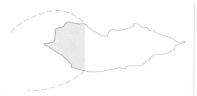

6

The West and the Outer Islands

…Men who emerged from the sea, from a sewn boat when the sea was flat calm.
They had swords and we had (only) sticks, and they were ready for a fight to the death.
Men who went up two passes: a single one was not large enough to take them.
Men who drank up the water of two springs: a single one was not enough to quench their thirst…

From an old Socotri poem about the pirates who visited
Socotra's coasts (translation by Miranda Morris)

Western Socotra really has only one attraction – or three attractions in one region – but what attractions they are! Shu'ab beach, accessible only by boat, must surely be one of the most beautiful in the world, while Detwah beach and lagoon (also stunning, and a protected nature sanctuary) are also full of interest, as is the neighbouring village of Qalansiyah. About 20km offshore from Qalansiyah is the sea-stack Sabuniya (page 157), an important nature sanctuary both for its marine life and for nesting birds, but turbulent seas make it hard to access. The Maalah cliffs and adjacent plateau between Qalansiyah and Shu'ab shelter Socotra's second highest diversity of species after the Haggeher mountains, not just plants and invertebrates but also reptiles.

The outer islands of Samha, Darsa and Abd el Kuri (page 154) are still intriguingly little known and surely ripe for increased tourism. At the time of writing, however, these islands are difficult, if not impossible, for tourists to visit. In particular Abd el Kuri, the largest and furthest island, was recently declared off-limits to tourists by Socotra's governor. The status of Samha and Darsa are less clear. They weren't possible to access when Chris and Miranda visited Socotra in March 2024, but there was also a sense of 'maybe soon' and 'wait and see'. Darsa is uninhabited (except by rats and seabirds) but the other two have small (very small) populations. There are no tourist facilities whatsoever at present. Back in 1898, at the time of the joint natural-history expedition to Socotra by the British and Liverpool Museums led by Henry Ogg Forbes, the team spent time collecting specimens in Abd el Kuri before continuing to Socotra. Much more recently, a few years ago when pirates were plying their unsavoury trade in and around the Arabian Sea, it's thought that some of them used the island as a base for their powerboats.

QALANSIYAH

Pronounced Kallan-*see*-yah with the emphasis on 'see', this is the second-largest town (or large village) on the island, head of the Qalansiyah district, and if you've been discouraged by the rubbish and general scruffiness of Hadiboh then you could find it refreshingly friendly and pleasant. About 75km west of Hadiboh, on a pretty good road, Qalansiyah is characterised by typical Socotri architecture of

Just as Socotra's dragon's blood trees are endangered both because grazing pressure inhibits natural regeneration and by climatic effects such as drought and cyclones, so too are its frankincense trees (*Boswellia*). The archipelago has several species, all unique, and all in the IUCN Red List. Much loved on Socotra for their local (ethnobotanical) use, the fragrant resins of these *Boswellia* are well known worldwide as olibanum. In the past few years, several local initiatives to protect them have popped up on the island. One such is Aziza Said Fadnhan's garden at Shata, near Qalansiyah, where – since witnessing the devastation caused by the 2015 cyclones – she has been replanting two species of *Boswellia* (*B elongata* and *B socotra*) together with *Aloe* and *Euphorbia* species from the area. Supported by the Socotra Al-Ata'a Foundation, the Environment Protection Authority of Socotra, UNDP/SGBP and the local communities, in 2016 **Aziza's Garden** became one of the largest *Boswellia* replantation sites on the island. Some of her trees derive from cuttings of *Boswellia* that were destroyed by the cyclones, others from seeds.

To arrange a visit to Aziza's garden (⊕ N12°40'03.5" E53°33'06.7"), ask your guide to contact the Environment Protection Authority staff on the island. For details of similar individual conservation projects by Socotri islanders, see page 88.

well-spaced houses built solidly from large blocks of the local stone. On some, this stonework has been done with great care to achieve a pleasing blend of natural colours, sometimes almost golden if the light is right. Wander down the wide streets and twisty alleys and you'll be greeted shyly by kids who – at least at this point – enjoy having their photos taken, and you can admire the painted doors which are so characteristic of Socotra. There is a market area, a few grocery and all-purpose shops (one sells good smoothies!) and a generally relaxed atmosphere.

Once just a traditional fishing village, Qalansiyah has a more affluent and cared-for feel to it nowadays and you could well spend a couple of nights or more here, to explore the lagoon, take a boat trip to beautiful Shu'ab (page 151), watch the coming and going of fishing boats, walk in the surrounding area or visit Aziza Said Fadnhan's garden (see above). At present the Detwah campsite (actually a row of campsites run by a mix of locals and tour companies, beautifully located along the shore) is the only accommodation, but it's possible some enterprising person will set up a homestay or guesthouse sooner or later.

Also in Qalansiyah, it used to be possible to arrange for a boat to take you to the outer islands of Samha, Darsa and, if you were really adventurous and planned further in advance, Abd el Kuri (page 154). At the time of writing, visiting these islands was prohibited, but check with your tour operator as there's every chance this situation will change again for at least some of the islands.

On the red rocks of the cliffs nearby you can find the bizarre *Dorstenia gigas* or Socotran fig, looking like something from a wizard's apothecary with its awkward swollen stem, as well as rare myrrhs and aloes and various other island endemics.

DETWAH BEACH AND LAGOON

This is one of Socotra's protected nature sanctuaries (page 163) and the lagoon was declared a Ramsar site in 2000. To quote from the Ramsar description:

The site is a coastal lagoon on the northwestern side of Socotra Island…consisting of a tidal inlet open to the sea, it is surrounded by sand dunes and 400m-high limestone and granite cliffs. The relatively pristine sea grass habitat provides ideal refuge from predators, acting as a feeding area and shelter for juvenile fish, and it is the only site on the island where the vulnerable leopard stingray (*Himantura uarnak*) and the near-threatened bluespotted ribbontail ray (*Taeniura lymma*) have been recorded. It is considered an important roosting and feeding area for waterbirds, with 32 species recorded of which ten are resident breeding species and 16 wintering species.

The view looking down on the beach and lagoon from above is one of the most famous in Socotra – so beautiful that we actually gasped! It was thus especially disappointing to find so much rubbish when we reached the bottom and started to set up camp. We whipped out our providently packed dustbin sacks and bags and, in full litter-pick mode, filled five of them, leaving ourselves with a pristine site (see photo, page 60). Some of the plastic bottles will have been washed in on the tide, but a miscellany of

THE BEST VIEWS OF DETWAH LAGOON

When viewed from near sea level it's easy to underestimate just how vast Detwah lagoon is, though if you walk from camp to even the closest point of ocean, you'll start to get some idea. There are at least four options to take in the astonishing views from higher up, depending on your activity preferences and budget.

The most common, almost obligatory, option is also the most straightforward, requiring just a few minutes' drive from Qalanisyah. You'll be driven past some old tanks near the beach-front and up to the headland at the lagoon's southwest corner. A very short walk from your parking spot takes you to a lookout with breathtaking views over the white sands and azure waters, made all the more impressive by it being most people's first sighting of Detwah.

The second option, and perhaps a good one for sunset, is to follow a dirt track up from your campsite for a few minutes to the small hills behind, where you'll have a view looking north across the lagoon.

For the more energetic and adventurous, Chris and Miranda recommend a sunrise hike up the high peak to the east of the camping area. You'll need a local guide for this as the path isn't always obvious or easy to follow, plus you'll likely drive the first part rather than hike all the way from camp. The route is mostly uphill and, like many in Socotra, can be a bit of a rocky scramble in the steeper parts, but after an hour or so of hiking you are richly rewarded by spectacular views of the lagoon laid out far below, along with Qalansiyah to the southwest. Take your time to enjoy the amazing variety of succulents on the peak and appreciate the kestrels and vultures circling around at eye level. The photo on the cover of this guide gives you some idea what to expect, as it was taken from up here.

The fourth, and most unique, possibility is by gyrocopter (page 54), though it requires a more expensive hour-long flight to make it there and back from your pickup point near the airport. Keep a sharp eye out for turtles, rays and other marine life in the waters below. There's even a chance of seeing whale sharks in the ocean to the north of the island while en-route to or from the lagoon.

It's hard to imagine how or why someone would pick an unattractive, grey/black and possibly rather smelly chunk of something-or-other off the beach or from the sea and decide that it was supremely valuable, but long ago it happened, and ambergris acquired its almost legendary reputation. Reportedly Ancient Greeks crumbled it into wine to speed up drunkenness, and Casanova added it to chocolate mousse as an aphrodisiac; while in the Middle Ages it was prescribed to treat everything from epilepsy to impotence, including warding off the odours believed to spread the Black Death. It has been called the 'treasure of the sea' and 'floating gold', and there's recent fossilised evidence of it dating back 1.75 million years.

Ambergris, ambergrease, or grey amber is, says Wikipedia, 'a solid, waxy, flammable substance of a dull grey or blackish colour produced in the digestive system of sperm whales' and, it is now believed, is expelled from their nether end, so it's not the 'whale vomit' it has sometimes been called. Its name comes from the Latin: *ambra grisea*, Old French: *ambre gris*, meaning 'grey amber'.

For many centuries its origin was a mystery. Maybe it flowed from undersea springs, or was the dung of a giant goose-shaped bird, or hardened sea foam...? Marco Polo claimed (from hearsay) that Socotra was a rich source; and Socotri legend tells of an ambergris tree in the dark depths of the ocean, guarded by *jinn* and attacked by huge hungry giant whales that grab what they can, dislodging chunks that then float to the surface. Tradition dictates that any Socotri finding a piece should give thanks to Allah before touching it and customarily he or she

other debris had been left by other campers and picnickers. In fact the local people do organise litter collections here too, and some tour operators are now joining in, but it's a big and ongoing problem which benefits from a bit of extra help.

A chain of campsites run along the south side of the lagoon, with several shared toilet and shower blocks available for everyone to use. The camping area here has grown significantly in the last few years and is undoubtedly one of the most popular locations on the island, but even so there is plenty of space to accommodate everyone.

What makes Detwah special, apart from its beauty and its scientific interest – and the campsites – is the chance to meet 'Ellai the Caveman' (pronounced 'Ah-lie-yah') and see his cave, which includes a whale jawbone and a complete dolphin skeleton (apart from its teeth, which are proudly strung on a necklace around Ellai's neck). He will delight in taking you on a marine-life tour of the eastern part of the shallow lagoon; it's the home of so many strange and marvellous creatures that seem to sit around in the hope of being photographed: we saw pufferfish, stingrays, sea cucumbers, octopus, squid – and much more. Given warning, Ellai will also collect and cook a lunch of local marine life but, for the sake of sustainability I'm not sure that the offer should be taken up.

Abdullah Ellai has a backstory which, with telling and re-telling, has almost become a part of Socotri folklore. He was born in the cave and was the third generation of his family to live there (now he lives mostly in Qalansiyah because his wife and several children prefer home comforts and his wife likes to watch TV); some years ago he found ambergris (see above) which made him briefly rich; he travelled to the mainland... What is absolutely clear, however, is that he loves Socotra, his cave, the lagoon and all the creatures in it, understands the natural world and is contented with his life. He is also very well attuned to the role he has

will keep only half, giving the rest away if need arises. Some Socotri villagers may occasionally 'harvest' it from the carcasses of beached whales, in which case most goes to whoever spotted the whale and the rest to those who assisted in stripping the meat and organs. But it's all too rare a find.

In reality…sperm whales are particularly partial to cephalopods like squid (such as you may see in Detwah lagoon) and cuttlefish, which have uncomfortably indigestible beaks; most of these get vomited out before digestion, but in about 1% of cases (it is thought) some continue to the intestine where they can get stuck and cause irritation. Fortunately both for the whales and for perfumiers worldwide, the whales can produce a kind of oily high-cholesterol slurry which encases the beaks; they bind together into a lump – ambergris – which is then excreted with faeces. Bobbing around in the ocean, it hardens into a kind of clayey state, said to feel slightly waxy as you hold it in your hands; the hardness increases (and its initial faecal smell decreases) as it ages, and its black-grey-brown-white colour changes.

Its role in the perfume industry is massive and it commands huge prices, with top houses such as Lanvin and Chanel using it both for its own scent and for its ability to enrich and prolong others. It can also be used in medicine and food, and one buyer in the Middle East grinds it up into milk and honey as an aphrodisiac. In the US its sale is illegal, because sperm whales are protected. To help you to identify that mysterious lump you may (you hope) find on the beach, check w ambergris.co.nz/identification.

acquired in tourism. Arrange through your guide to meet him and you will find a delightful and charming man, probably about 60 but as agile as a goat, with a deep knowledge of his environment and an eagerness to share it. We know about the agility first hand. I (Hilary) was wearing old sandals which I had brought for wading in the lagoon. I hadn't realised that the climb to Ellai's cave was just that – a climb – so long before we'd got to the steepest part my sandal strap broke. I was in a strop – I couldn't see how I was going to walk back to the campsite, let alone continue to the cave or explore the lagoon. Then we (Janice had stayed with me for moral support) spied this brown figure bounding barefoot down the mountain side. It was Ellai. He explained that he knew every rock on that hillside so could leap around safely. Within minutes he had found a piece of wire and some discarded string and, together with our guide's help and a strip torn off Janice's beach towel, did a superb repair job and I was able to continue the tour. The rest of our group were shown the various curiosities in and around his cave and given a small snack of seafood.

So, assuming you will visit Ellai, because most visitors do, come equipped both for the short climb up to the cave and for exploring the lagoon. For oldies like us that means sturdy shoes or boots (it is a steep climb, with some rock scrambling) a hiking pole for the climb ('yes', says Janice), and sandals (not flip-flops) for walking in the lagoon.

THE LAGOON This is the high spot of the Qalansiyah area, although from the marine animal welfare point of view it made us a bit uneasy. It is best explored at low tide when all the life just below the surface is easily visible, but there is not much variation in depth between high and low so even high tide doesn't go much above your knees. Be wary of stingrays, of which there are many and which impart a dramatically painful sting from their tails if disturbed or stepped on. Adopting

Qalansiyah (Chris Miller)

1–5 About 75km west of Hadiboh, Qalansiyah is considered by most visitors to be refreshingly friendly and pleasant when compared with the capital. Wander the wide streets and twisty alleyways to soak up the laidback atmosphere. The buildings are in typical Socotri style, built from rough-cut local stone. The locals – especially the kids – are generally relaxed about being photographed, but you should always ask their permission (page 137)

1 Simon Urwin, *2 & 3* Chris Miller, *4 & 5* Nicole Smoot

145

1 The lookout over Detwah beach and lagoon (page 138) (Nicole Smoot)

2 Returning from Ellai's cave through Detwah lagoon (Hilary Bradt)

3, 4 & 5 One of the things that makes Detwah special is the chance to meet 'Ellai the Caveman'. He'll take you on a tour of the lagoon's marine life, possibly including fast swimming stingrays or even a friendly octopus (page 140)

3 Simon Urwin, *4 & 5* Nicole Smoot

1 Extraordinary rock formations and colours en route to Shu'ab (page 151) (Chris Miller)

2 A local fisherman bringing home a stingray from Detwah lagoon (Chris Miller)

3 A western reef heron on the pink rocks, as seen from the boat ride to Shu'ab (Chris Miller)

4 Spinner dolphins often accompany boats heading for Shu'ab (Nicole Smoot)

5, 6 & 7 The boat trip to Shu'ab beach — surely one of the most beautiful in the world — is enjoyed as much by the camp team as by the passengers. The colour and patterns of the rocks are as special as the destination (5 & 7 Hilary Bradt, 6 Nicole Smoot)

Camping at Shu'ab beach (Chris Miller)

the 'stingray shuffle' will alert the creatures to your presence, but also stirs up the sand and clouds the water. On our exploration we were shown a puffer fish whose trembling lips when held up for the photographers still worry us, a squid which squirted ink and an octopus which Ellai said was his friend. It arrived so conveniently to be shown off to us that one of our group commented, 'I think he and the octopus have an arrangement.'

We also saw sea cucumbers, a swimming cowrie and a prehistoric-looking chiton. Emily Glover comments: 'The lagoon is interesting for it is one of the few sheltered intertidal habitats on the island, with sea grass patches, coralline algae and seaweeds with a diversity of invertebrates including molluscs, some of which are edible or have other value including large numbers of living money cowrie. Abundant mussels and rock oysters are part of the local diet.'

Chris waded across the sandy southwestern part of the lagoon, where there is less marine life, for a swim in the sea. This is quite an undertaking (it took him about 40 minutes) and is perhaps not best practice because of damage to the marine life in the lagoon, but rewarding for the swim and the birds. Alternatively you can follow the lagoon shoreline around and stay on the sand to get to the ocean which will take a bit longer, but avoids any risk of being stung by the rays. Chris saw whimbrel and Eurasian curlew – both migrant waders – and you could also expect to see turnstones, plovers, greenshanks and little stints. This is also a great area for seeing both colour variations of the western reef heron: more commonly grey but you may also see a white morph. The lagoon is also one of the best places to spot a visiting osprey.

SHU'AB BEACH

The boat trip to this beach is definitely a highlight of any trip to Socotra and is normally a scheduled part of the local tour operators' one-week and two-week itineraries. On a fine day – and you can only do it on a reasonably calm day – everything about it is perfect. The boats are colourful, the fishing rewarding (expect fresh fish for dinner), the jutting pink cliffs extraordinary, the seabirds plentiful, and the sea such a brilliant blue-green that we thought we were looking at some exotic gull flying close to the water until we realised that its greenish breast was a reflection of the sea. There is a resident pod of spinner dolphins and, although they may not give you a display of spinning, they will happily play around your boat.

Birders will have a wonderful time identifying the birds nesting (or resting) on the cliffs. Expect to see brown boobies and Socotra cormorants, and flying around are sooty gulls and great crested terns. Further out to sea, if you're very lucky, you might see a masked booby, Persian shearwaters and Jouanin's petrel.

And that's just the boat trip. Shu'ab actually does have road access too, but it's a suspension-challenging 3-hour drive from the turn-off from the main coast road and goes to the village at the southern end of the beach. This is some 3 miles from the area where the boat drops you so the sands at the northern end are pristine, and this must surely be one of the most beautiful beaches in the world. At the high tide line are smooth, colourful little pebbles like remnants from a jewellery maker's workshop.

The beach is also great for ghost crabs and an assortment of gulls and waders. Sometimes, also, you can see the spinner dolphins performing out at sea.

Most people take a boat out to Shu'ab first thing in the morning, returning to Qalansiyah later that day. If you have the time, it is also possible to enjoy the beach at a more relaxed pace by camping there overnight, where you'll probably have a local or two join you to share stories over dinner and try to convince you to give them your mask and snorkel if you thought to bring one with you. Note there are no bathroom facilities here, and camping might cost you extra, as the boat driver is likely to be paid double for an overnight stay.

There is a wreck about 2km offshore that is great for diving (page 55). For snorkelling, just enter the water near the north end of the beach and follow the coast back towards Qalansiyah as far as you like before turning back to the beach again; you should find plenty to see, especially if you dive down a couple of metres to see what's happening under the various rock overhangs you'll pass by.

The weather changed for our return boat ride to Qalansiyah, revealing a quite different ocean – slate grey and ominous, with a sharp wind whipping waves and spray into the boat so that we arrived thoroughly soaked. It gave us a very small idea of what Socotra's stormy season must be like.

THE OUTER ISLANDS *Julian Jansen van Rensburg*

Note that at the time of writing, tourists were not permitted to visit the outer islands, likely as a result of a military base being built by the UAE on the largest island, Abd

---

PROTECTIVE LAWS AND REGULATIONS *Alan Forrest*

Detwah lagoon is listed as a **Ramsar Site** – the only one on the Socotra archipelago – under the Convention on Wetlands of International Importance especially as Waterfowl Habitat 1971, but this listing unfortunately confers no protection by law. The same is true of much of the rest of Socotra's natural world, which benefits – theoretically – from a large amount of other protection listed below, much of which unfortunately confers no legally enforceable measures.

1. **Socotra Conservation Zoning Plan** (page 163), under which Detwah is classed as a **Nature Sanctuary**. This plan defines, for each zone, what is allowed and what is not, and also lists more general articles that are important for the entire archipelago. These are not simply guidelines – the Zoning Plan is an actual local *law*, applicable to both islanders and visitors. Nature Sanctuaries have the highest level of protection within the plan because they contain highly vulnerable species, and even ecotourism infrastructure is not allowed.

2. **UNESCO World Heritage Site** – UNESCO Convention concerning the Protection of the World Cultural and Natural Heritage, 1972. This highlights the island's globally unique and significant natural heritage, but confers no legal protection. UNESCO itself has no power or capacity to enforce or provide protection; this is ultimately a local responsibility, which visitors can be encouraged to join the islanders in observing. If, however, it is not carried out satisfactorily, the island's heritage status can be withdrawn.

3. **UNESCO Convention for the Safeguarding of the Intangible Cultural Heritage** (ICH), 2003. This convention is not well known on Socotra although it is perhaps one of the conventions most relevant for the island. It covers both the Socotri language and other autochthonous ICH, including handicrafts and games, some of which could well be added to UNESCO's various ICH inventories in the future.

4. **UNESCO MAB Reserve** – UNESCO Man and the Biosphere Programme, 1971. Protects nothing by law, but is yet another indication of the area's importance.

el Kuri, and where there is still a lot of ongoing construction taking place. Why all the islands are off-limits is less clear, and when Chris and Miranda visited Socotra in March 2024 there seemed to be some optimism that the smaller islands might be possible to visit again soon. The information that follows was written before the restrictions were put in place, but if you are hoping to visit any of the islands please check with your tour company to find out what the latest situation is, and whether a visit is even possible.

To the south of Socotra and lying further west towards Africa are the archipelago's three other islands: Samha and Darsa (known as 'The Brothers' from the dragon's-blood-tree legend that the blood flowed from two brothers who fought each other to the death – a more prosaic alternative to the version where a dragon was slain by an elephant) and Abd el Kuri. In terms of flora and fauna these have been less extensively explored than Socotra itself and no doubt have further surprises waiting to be revealed, but already a number of their own endemic species have been recorded.

The Brothers can be reached by local fishing boat from Qalansiyah, but only when the weather is favourable. The journey takes several hours; it's quite arduous and very expensive. Ask your guide beforehand to make enquiries for you. Don't be tempted to skimp on quality for the sake of cost: be sure to pick a boat with two

5. **UNESCO Convention on the Protection of the Underwater Cultural Heritage**, 2001. This might have given at least some (moral) protection to the many shipwrecks around Socotra, but it has not yet been ratified by Yemen.

6. **Important Bird and Biodiversity Areas – BirdLife International**. This classification highlights the most important sites for bird diversity, but again protects nothing by law.

7. The **Yemen Environment Law No.26** specifies a range of prohibited activities in terms of damage, degradation and transportation of wildlife that lives in Yemen. The removal of any wildlife or wildlife products requires special permission from the relevant authorities. This law is in response to the Convention on Biological Diversity (1992).

8. **CITES** – Convention on International Trade in Endangered Species of Wild Fauna and Flora, 1973. Has nothing unique to Socotra, but several plant groups are included – all species of *Aloe* on Appendix II, all species of orchids on Appendix II, all succulent species of euphorbia on Appendix II. Also the Socotra buzzard *Buteo socotrensis* and Socotra chameleon *Chameleo monachus* are on Appendix II, which means trade must be controlled so it is compatible with species survival.

9. The **cultural heritage of Yemen** is protected by national legislation forbidding the trading or the free disposal of movable archaeological objects and the export of movable archaeological objects unless a temporary permission is given by the authorities. Yemeni authorities will ask for the retrieval and the repatriation of illegally exported objects. Yemen has also ratified the 1954 Hague Convention for the **Protection of Cultural Property in the Event of Armed Conflict**, but this largely gives responsibility to the national government and there has never (yet) been a prosecution by the International Criminal Court for the destruction of cultural property.

6

outboard engines or one that is in good repair, owing to the strong currents and seas that you will encounter; and do heed the advice of the fishermen who will take you out. They understand local conditions and, even if the sea looks calm from Qalansiyah beach, it can become very rough further offshore. You can get to The Brothers and back in a day, but it's best to take some basic overnight gear just in case the weather suddenly worsens; there are no facilities for tourists, but you can ask to camp on Samha. On a calm day it can be a lovely trip; you may spot spinner dolphins, as well as terns, herons, brown boobies, Socotra cormorants and various gulls. If you come close enough to the cliffs, look out (in season) for birds nesting. It's likely that your boatman will also take the opportunity to catch some fish on the way, with a line set up at the stern; they are plentiful in these waters, and you may sometimes see shoals of them frothing the surface.

SAMHA This is a desertic island, about 11km long by 5km across, dominated by a flat-topped limestone plateau. It has ten endemic plant species (found only on this island), with eight of them restricted to the small area of cliffs on the escarpment that catch the monsoon fog and mist. These include *Begonia samhaensis* and *Pelargonium insularis,* both well-known groups globally.

There is one anchorage point, next to the only village on the island. From this village it is possible, with a guide, to walk along the coastline or up to the escarpment, where the views of Socotra can be fantastic. The village is crammed into a small bay, with a school and mosque at the entrance and a group of tightly clustered square stone houses that extend to the base of a hill. The school does not always function, as it's normal for teachers not to stay long at such a remote location. It's a desperately poor village, whose people are either stuck there for the duration of the monsoon season or else migrate to the mainland during this time.

You could probably camp, with permission, to the west on the beach, or in the mountainous interior if you want to trek there, or overnight stays with the local fishermen could possibly be arranged. The people are friendly to visitors. In return you could offer cash (discuss with your guide), or bring enough food to share, or give something for the school, or donate basic first-aid equipment as they have no medical facilities.

DARSA Samha and its eastern neighbour Darsa are excellent bird-watching sites, with a good chance of seeing masked and brown booby, red-billed tropicbird, Persian shearwater, sooty gull, bridled tern, Saunders' tern and common noddy. Birds are particularly dense on Darsa and you can hear the cacophony as you approach. On one side of the islet is a sand dune where you can disembark, but you should not walk up to the cliffs as this will disturb the many nesting birds. The island is tiny and steep, about 6km long by 2km broad, uninhabited, and overnighting there is, according to those that have tried, not recommended. This is due to the large number of rats that also inhabit the island and feed off the birds' eggs and young, and possibly also any stray tourists that may turn up.

ABD EL KURI This larger island is a further 60km to the west, just 80km from Cape Guardafui on the coast of Somalia, and is a major expedition in terms of travelling time and cost. While there is a weekly flight from Socotra airport to Abd el Kuri, it is strictly locals only – presumably intended for those working on the construction taking place there. This means any visit, assuming it is allowed at all, will be via a long and difficult boat journey. You need to discuss any potential visit with your tour operator well before leaving home to make sure that it will be practicable at the time you choose, or pick a tour operator that already has it in one of their itineraries. Utterly remote, Abd el Kuri is the subject of tales that include pirates (both historical and present-day), shipwrecks and unmanageably stormy seas. Even local fishermen get into difficulties, and for several months of the year it's largely inaccessible. Also a desertic island and quite different in character from Socotra and the other islands, it is around 32km long and 6km wide and dominated by the mountain Jebel Saleh (509m), with a fluctuating estimated population of around 400 inhabitants from various racial origins. Very little fresh water is available. The island has 15 endemic plants, including the unusual tree *Euphorbia abdelkuri*, which has been described as

JUST SO SOCOTRA

This Uninhabited Island
Is off Cape Gardafui,
By the Beaches of Socotra
And the Pink Arabian Sea;
But it's hot – too hot from Suez
For the likes of you and me
Ever to go
In a P. and O.
And call on the Cake-Parsee!

Just So Stories, Rudyard Kipling, 1902

The Cake-Parsee, as *Just So Stories* fans will know, is in *How the Rhinoceros got his Skin*, and this is not Kipling's only allusion to Socotra. Earlier in the story he refers to 'the Exclusively Uninhabited Interior which abuts on the islands of Mazanderan, Socotra, and the Promontories of the Larger Equinox', and his poem *The Junk and the Dhow*, published in 1926, contains the line 'From Socotra to Selankhor of the windlass and the anchor.'

Born in India in 1865, Kipling lived there (apart from a brief visit to England aged three) until he was six and was sent to England for schooling. He went back to India as a young man in 1882 and stayed, working on local English-language newspapers, until 1889, when he returned to England and, in 1892, got married 'in the thick of an influenza epidemic, when the undertakers had run out of black horses and the dead had to be content with brown ones.' At the end of that year his much-loved daughter Josephine (known as Effie) was born. Kipling used to tell the little girl stories which she insisted should always be repeated 'just so', without any deviation from the previous telling. Sadly she died aged six in 1899, and in 1902 Kipling's collection of stories – the *Just So Stories* – was published, containing so many images and memories linked to his years in India.

Travelling between England and India, Kipling must at some point have sailed (as in the poem) on a P. and O. passenger liner from Suez, passing by Socotra with its beaches and its 'uninhabited islands'. In the *Just So Stories* he is simply having fun with names rather than sticking to geography, but Abd el Kuri, which indeed is located between Cape Guardafui (on the tip of Somalia) and Socotra, does seem likely to have inspired the island where the Cake-Parsee lives. On the other hand, Kipling's own sketch of his imaginary island looks more like little Darsa's craggy peak. Either way, it seems that the Socotra archipelago has a presence in 20th-century children's literature!

the most remarkable species of euphorbia in the world and has a toxic latex that should be avoided – as it is by livestock. Being so much closer to Africa than the other islands, there are differences in its flora even from Socotra. Other endemics include the Abd el Kuri sparrow (*Passer hemileucus*) and the Socotran wall lizard *Mesalina kuri*. The 1898 zoological and botanical expedition of the British and Liverpool museums, set up by Henry Ogg Forbes, called in to collect specimens from Abd el Kuri first before continuing to Socotra, and got a good haul. In only a small area, to paraphrase Forbes:

> Birds were disappointingly few, but of the species we obtained two proved to be new to science, a sparrow and a wagtail. Two species of lizard were also found to be new. Land shells were abundant under stones and upon the bushes, and of these four are unknown elsewhere. Very few butterflies – only three all told – beetles or bees were observed, but of the two latter groups all the species turned out to be undescribed, while one of the beetles forms the type of a new genus.

Abd el Kuri shipwrecks Over the years many ships have run into difficulties here, as the seas around the islands can be savage. One shipwreck meticulously recorded by one of its officers was that of the British cargo ship **SS *Ayrshire***, the flagship of the British Clan Line fleet, on 23 March 1965. Heading from Liverpool to Brisbane, after passing through the Suez Canal she hit rocks off Abd el Kuri 'with a tremendous crunch' and was badly damaged; three lifeboats were launched, carrying passengers, provisions and most of the ship's company, leaving just a small skeleton crew on board. The captain then quickly and deliberately headed for the nearest beach (about four miles away) and ran her aground before she could sink.

The officer recorded the ship's first approach:

> The island was a striking sight with its barren red mountains towering over us. The whole coastline was sheer except for a sandy bay halfway along the southern coast. No-one thought anything was special about this little beach with its brilliant white sand, but very soon it would probably save a few lives.

Indeed, it was where the *Ayrshire* rammed ashore, thus saving her cargo, which included cars, carpets, machinery, lino, ceramic tiles, 150 tons of bagged salt and… 1,500 bags of mothballs. The little crew on board were safe, and the fourth lifeboat set off to locate the other three in the darkness and guide them back, after which the officer recorded 'By 23.00 all were back on board and time for a beer!'

Remember that the islands were still a part of Britain's Aden Protectorate, so reaction to the accident was thoroughly British. Nearby vessels kept in contact, as did the authorities in Aden, and the seven passengers were taken off within days by a Clan Line sister ship. Attempts to repair the *Ayrshire* continued well into April, cadets and officers all mucking in together, while various vessels came and went to retrieve as much cargo as possible and insurance assessors took photos and tutted over the damage. The men lived on board, had ample provisions, played football on the beach and generally survived well. On 11 April, the officer records, a helicopter suddenly hovered overhead, a man was winched down on a wire and…he delivered the morning papers. However, the damage eventually proved to have been too serious for the ship to be repaired and towed away; on 29 April the men on board were transported to Aden and the *Ayrshire* was abandoned, after having its funnel's insignia blacked out 'so as not to be a bad advertisement.' (For more of the officer's account see w wrecksite.eu/wreck.aspx?204360.)

The three outer islands and two stacks mentioned in this chapter weren't enough for 17th-century French cartographer Alain Manesson Mallet (1630–1706): on the 1683 map of 'Zocotora' in his five-volume *Description de l'Univers* he also shows two quite substantial islands off the northern coast. Interestingly, he has Samha and Darsa, today often called The Brothers, neatly positioned off the south coast but named Isles des Soeurs (sisters); while Abd el Kuri, a recognisable shape but shown off the west coast at about the level of Shu'ab, has smaller islands (presumably the stacks) to its north and south – and these three are named Isles Masculinas ou des Frères (brothers). Quite a family affair! – or possibly, given the storminess of the sea, *liaisons dangereuses*?

A less gentle shipwreck was that of the Somali vessel ***Mariam IV*** in July 2006; she sank in a storm off Abd el Kuri and tragically six of the crew members died. The remaining 13 were rescued by a German helicopter a week later but the chief officer was mistakenly left behind, and the weather and communications were so bad that he could not be picked up and taken back to mainland Yemen for a further two months. He described the island as, 'a hellish place, where time stands still, and one can feel completely alone in the world.'

SEA STACKS

The Socotra archipelago also includes several uninhabited sea stacks, of which the best known are **Kal Farun** (about 21km north of the western end of Abd el Kuri) and **Sabuniya**, about 20km west of Qalansiyah, occasionally nicknamed Pharaoh's Balls. These stacks are important nature sanctuaries both for their marine life and for nesting birds. The treacherous seas make them difficult, and potentially dangerous, to reach, but the trip to Sabuniya can offer some of Socotra's best seabird sightings. Speak to your guide about hiring a fishing boat from Qalansiyah for the typically 1½-hour journey offshore. Depending on the time of year, you can enjoy excellent sightings of red-billed tropicbirds, Socotra cormorants, Persian shearwaters, Jouanin's petrels, brown noddies and both brown and masked boobies. Additionally, the waters around these islands are rich in marine mammals, including dolphins, making the trip even more rewarding.

The sea directly around the shores of all three of these outer islands and the sea stacks is designated a '**national park**' under the archipelago's Marine Conservation Zoning Plan of 2000, which allows for protection relevant to that status. Additionally, on Abd el Kuri, Samha and the whole of Darsa there are areas with higher protected status designated '**nature sanctuaries**'. For more on this see pages 92 and 163.

Appendix 1

BOOKS
Background reading

Islands of Heritage: Conservation and Transformation in Yemen Peutz, Nathalie; Stanford University Press, 2018. This very substantial ethnography is packed with knowledgeable information, from Socotra's language, history, heritage and politics to its roads, goats and kitchen gardens. And above all its people. Nathalie Peutz lived and researched on the island, and strikes a careful balance between the human and the academic. Much of the information is too intensive for it to be a quick read, but no other book will give you such a complete and colourful picture of 21st-century Socotra and its recent history.

Socotra: A Natural History of the Islands and their People ed Cheung, Catherine & DeVantier, Lyndon; Odyssey Books & Guides, 2006. A massive and encyclopaedic 396-page volume, beautifully presented and illustrated, with information about pretty much every aspect of the archipelago, from records of its ancient history, people and culture to extensive sections on its wildlife and natural world. Its Science Editor Kay Van Damme has also written pieces for this Bradt guide, as have contributors Miranda Morris and Julian Jansen van Rensburg. It is available secondhand, but at very high (three-figure) prices.

Culture/natural world

A Comparative Cultural Glossary across the Modern South Arabian Language Family Morris, Miranda; Watson, Janet C E; Eades & Domenyk; Manchester University (Journal of Semitic Studies Supplement), 2019. The result of collaborative work conducted with a number of native speakers of the languages, this presents a comparative cultural glossary of 345 head terms, which are given in the six Modern South Arabian languages including Socotri.

Birds of the Horn of Africa Redman, Nigel, Stevenson, Terry & Fanshawe, John; Princeton Field Guides, 2016. A fully revised and updated new edition of the acclaimed field guide to the 1,000+ species of resident, migrant, and vagrant birds found in northeast Africa, covering Ethiopia, Eritrea, Djibouti, Somalia and the Socotra archipelago. Includes the latest information on distribution, identification and taxonomy.

Birds of the Middle East Porter, Richard; Campbell, Oscar; Al-Sirhan, AbdulRahman; Helm Field Guide, 2024. The new third edition of this authoritative book covers more than 895 species recorded in the Middle East, including details of all regular visitors and breeding species. Featuring 180 stunning colour plates by three of the world's leading bird illustrators, this practical guide also includes concise species accounts describing key identification features, status, range, habitat and voice with fully updated distribution maps for each species. The essential field guide for anyone visiting the Middle East, and covering all the birds of Socotra.

Botany of Socotra Balfour, Isaac Bayley; General Books LLC, Memphis, USA. A 2012 version of Balfour's 1880 report, created using optical character-recognition software. Balfour gives a comprehensive listing of species as he found them (enough of the accompanying descriptions are in Latin to be irritating to non-Latin scholars), together with some useful explanatory background and observations about the island.

Ethnoflora of the Soqotra Archipelago Miller, Anthony G & Morris, Miranda; Royal Botanic Gardens Edinburgh, 2004. A massive, 758-page book describing and illustrating all 820 of Socotra's plant species, along with photos of most of the endemics. What makes it an exceptional and fascinating book for anyone with an interest in Socotra's plants and culture is the detailed descriptions of the traditional use each plant has to the Socotri people. Wherever there is a description in this Bradt guide of traditional plant uses, the information is derived from this book. As the cover blurb says, it 'bridges the gap between biologists and conservationists' and does it beautifully.

Island Voices: The Oral Art of Soqotra Morris, Miranda & Tanuf Nuh Il-Kishin; Brill, Leiden (Netherlands), 2021. This book presents over a thousand poems and songs, prayers, lullabies, work-chants, messages in code, riddles, examples of community wisdom encapsulated in poetic couplets, and stories centred on a short poem or exchange of poems. These were documented by oral transmission directly to the authors, or through recordings collected by them, in collaboration with Socotrans from all parts of the island. They are presented in Socotri (transcribed phonetically in Roman and in Arabic script), and in English and Arabic translation.

Maritime Traditions of the Fishermen of Socotra, The Jansen van Rensburg, Julian; Archaeopress Archaeology, Oxford, 2016. This book covers more than its title suggests, because the background to local fishery includes the history, geography, culture and traditions of a whole area. As well as the boats and equipment used, species caught, seasonal calendar of activities, fishing economy and so forth, the book also – probably uniquely – spotlights the lives of fishing families and communities in Socotra and tiny Samha Island.

Natural History of Sokotra and Abd-el-Kuri, The Forbes, Henry O & Ogilvie-Grant W R; Liverpool Museums, 1903. The original 1903 illustrated edition, edited by Henry O Forbes and published (all 700-odd pages of it) as a 'Special Bulletin' by the Liverpool Museums, is available to read and/or download online. A digitally reconstructed version was published in 2018 by London-based Forgotten Books (w forgottenbooks.com). It contains painstaking details of the flora, fauna and geology of these islands as encountered by a joint research team from the British Museum and the Liverpool Museums, led by Henry Forbes, together with a short 'Narrative of the Journey' and some enjoyable old photos and drawings.

Socotra's Special Birds Porter, Richard; Royal Society for the Conservation of Nature, 2023. This book covers the 50 species of birds that are special to the Socotra archipelago. They include the endemics, those with internationally important populations, the globally threatened species and a selection of those most likely to be seen. There is a section on the best places to watch birds and, at the end, a checklist of all the species recorded.

Travel

Island of the Dragon's Blood Botting, Douglas; Steve Savage Publishers, 2006. This authoritative, comprehensive, well-researched and entertainingly written travel narrative has become a classic. Botting's 1956 expedition to Socotra was the first serious survey since 1899 so there was plenty to discover and record, which he does with insight and affection for the place and its people.

Memoir on the Island of Socotra Wellsted J R; Isha Books (India), 2013. A digitally reissued version of the 1834 report by 26-year-old Lieutenant James Wellsted of the East India Company's Marine Service. Sent to check out Socotra as a possible naval coaling station, he diligently surveys as much as possible of the island, overcoming problems (recalcitrant local guides, non-availability of camels and more) with good sense and good humour, and produces a detailed and entertaining report. The downside is that it lacks an index.

Yemen: the Bradt Guide McLaughlin, Daniel; Bradt Guides, 2007. While we were researching the first edition in 2020, we saw tourists (from Thailand) immersed in Daniel's guide, despite its age; and indeed much of the material on Yemen – particularly its history – is still valid and very comprehensive. His chapter on Socotra shows that the island has changed quite a bit in the past 17 years. The book is a helpful travelling companion for its background to Yemen, still available (although not in great quantities) secondhand.

Yemen, Travels in Dictionary Land Mackintosh-Smith, Tim; Picador, 1999. Originally published by John Murray. There is only one chapter about Socotra – *Chapter 8, The Ancient Naturals* – but it's a delight, full of wit, humanity, sharp observation, enjoyment and love for the place. Of the book as a whole, the *Economist* reviewer commented: 'He loves the language as much as the landscape, the people as much as the extravagant history of the place' – and it's true. Second-hand copies aren't all that easy to find in the UK (more in US).

Miscellaneous

Socotra Sparrow, The Frank K Myers. A warning – despite an appealing picture of a Socotra sparrow on the cover, this rather lumpy spy story has no connection whatever with Socotra! The title seems to refer to one character once 'singing like a Socotra sparrow', slang for spilling the beans.

ACADEMIC PAPERS AND ARTICLES There's no shortage of academic material on Socotra, as you will quickly discover once you embark on an internet search. It's impracticable for us to list all the authors, but we suggest you start with those whose contributions feature most in this book; they all cover several fields and know the island extremely well: **Julian Jansen van Rensburg**, **Miranda Morris**, **Kay Van Damme** and **Alan Forrest**. Their details are on page vi, together with **Richard Porter** (birds) and **Raquel Vasconcelos** (reptiles), and between them they offer you a massive amount of relevant – and fascinating – background reading.

Among one author's favourites is Julian Jansen van Rensburg's 2018 *Rock Art of Soqotra, Yemen: A Forgotten Heritage*, available as a PDF, a comprehensive illustrated review of historical and current rock art research on the island which reveals some of its amazing ancient treasures. You may also enjoy: *What We Know and What We Do Not Know about Dragon Trees* (Petr Madera, Alan Forrest et al, 2020). The title says it all!

National Geographic magazine has published good articles on Socotra over the years, as has **Birdlife International** (w birdlife.org).

VIDEOS AND WEBSITES

Videos (including YouTube) Be a little cautious here – a few videos (particularly on YouTube) claim to be of Socotra, but include uncaptioned shots of the Yemen mainland including ornate buildings and city streets, which (if they were of Socotra) would make it a very different place. But there are stunning views as well, so keep looking. Videos by **National Geographic** are good, and we also recommend:

w **youtube.com/watch?v=XYFJtRnvSZQ**
For a description of the work of the Soqotra Heritage Project.
w **youtube.com/watch?v=Chkro9-ITYM**
Documentary giving a feel for life on the island.

w **youtube.com/watch?v=Ga4DncsyZj8**
Scenic views of Socotra.
w **youtube.com/watch?v=PJGQNcj7vzg**
For insight into traditional Socotri handicrafts.

Websites There is no shortage of these! Be careful of spellings when you search: some have So**Q**otra with a Q and others So**C**otra with a C, although most searches will bring up both. Some useful ones are:

w **adventuresoflilnicki.com** Nicole (page vi) blogs about off-the-beaten-path destinations with a strong focus on Yemen & Socotra. Helpful, practical & up-to-date information for travellers, & she also runs tours to Socotra & elsewhere.
w **bbc.com/travel/article/20211209-the-hermit-of-socotra-island** BBC article about Ellai the Caveman (page 140).
w **friendsofsoqotra.org** Helpful sections on the country & its wildlife, also hints for visitors.
w **inertianetwork.com** Very good Socotra section, with background, politics & tourist attractions.

w **nationalgeographic.com/podcasts/ overheard/article/episode-3-why-war-zones-need-science** Searching for traces of the earliest known humans to leave Africa.
w **osme.org/2020/04/checklist-of-the-birds-of-the-socotra-archipelago**
w **soqotraculturalheritage.org** Good background to the country & links to other info.
w **theconversation.com/socotra-archipelago-why-the-emiratis-have-set-their-sights-on-the-arab-worlds-garden-of-eden-218848** Coverage of the UAE presence on Socotra.

Appendix 2

LANGUAGE

With thanks to **Radwan Mobarak Ali Mohamed** of Socotra Eco-Tours who has provided this material and has more on the Eco-tours website **w** socotra-eco-tours. com.

ENGLISH	ARABIC	SOCOTRI
Yes	*Naam*	*Aha*
No	*La*	*La*
Please	*Argok*	*Farhabk*
Excuse me	*Afwan*	*Almadkak*
What is your name? (m)	*Aish Asmk*	*Fo Mak Sham*
What is your name? (f)	*Aish Asmk*	*Fo Mash Sham*
My name is…	*Asmi…*	*Manhi Sham…*
Hello	*Marhaba*	*Algaork*
Goodbye	*Me assalama*	*Meraʾah de allah*
Thank you	*Shukran*	*Yala bak allah*
You're welcome	*Afwan*	*Wa bak*
Let's go!	*Yallah!*	*Yallah!*
Stop, finish, enough	*Khalas*	*Khalas*
Breakfast	*Fatoor*	*Qazhim*
Lunch	*Ghada*	*Fkhio*
Dinner	*Asha*	*Tadeemo*
Water	*Maʾa*	*Reeho*
Car	*Seyyara*	*Seyyara*
Tent	*Khaima*	*Khaima*
Boat	*Qarab*	*Ghadfa*
Do you have…?	*Fi…?*	*Eno…?*
Fish	*Samak/Sayd*	*Souda*
Bread	*Khobz*	*Azhiro*
Honey	*Asal*	*Asal*
Dates	*Tmar*	*Tamar*
Milk	*Halib/Laban*	*Shahaf*
How much is that?	*Bkam Hada*	*Bkam Ahda*
That's very nice!	*Enho Altif Gadn*	*Shakar Bana/Mahser Bana*
That's beautiful! (view)	*Enho Gamil*	*Shakar*
Do you speak English?	*Hal Tkalam Englizi*	*Tshmotal Englizi*
I don't speak Arabic/Socotri	*Lan Atkalam Arabi/Socotri*	*Al Ashmotal Arabi/Socotri*

Appendix 3

SOCOTRA NATURE – PROTECTED BY LAW   *Dr Kay Van Damme*

The Socotra archipelago has been a Man and the Biosphere Reserve since 2003 and a UNESCO natural World Heritage Site since 2008. Most UNESCO sites (globally) are cultural rather than natural, and Socotra is one of only a few natural UNESCO sites in the Arab World. These global designations include a certain international protection for naturally sensitive areas, defined as the core property. However, even before Socotra was so designated, protection had already been established at national level, under one of Yemen's main national environmental laws – the **Socotra Conservation Zoning Plan**, also known as Presidential Decree n° 275 of year 2000. This national law then formed the basis for the delineation of the core and buffer areas of the UNESCO World Heritage Property, whose boundaries are exactly the same as those defined in the Zoning Plan.

Within the archipelago this plan (in two parts, terrestrial and marine) defines zones with different levels of protection, as follows and as shown on the map:

General Use Zone Located within the resource use reserve. Includes sites where a significant level of habitat modification has occurred and is designated for appropriate general development purposes.

Resource Use Reserve An area managed to ensure long-term protection of the unique biological diversity of the Socotra islands while providing both a sustainable flow of natural products and services to meet community needs and appropriate development activities.

National Park Natural areas of land or sea designated to protect the ecological integrity of the unique ecosystems of the Socotra islands for present and future generations, and to provide a foundation for scientific, educational and recreational opportunities as well as the appropriate development activities for ecotourism. Contains self-explanatory 'areas of special botanical interest'.

Nature Sanctuaries Areas of land or sea characterised by rare plant or animal species that still retain their natural character and are set aside for scientific research.

The **General Use Zones** or development zones, such as the urban areas Hadiboh and Qalansiyah and the harbour area at Hawlaf, have the relatively lowest (but not absent!) levels of protection. Sustainable development is allowed here to some extent, as long as it does not jeopardise the surrounding protected areas; they comprise almost all the rest of Socotra, with 72.6% of the total land surface designated as a national park and 23.5% as a nature reserve.

The **National Park** area, which includes the plateaux and mountains, corresponds entirely to the core zone of the World Heritage (WH) Property, so has a high protection status – anything threatening biodiversity here is in breach of both national and international agreements. Within the National Park area, there are several *terrestrial* **Nature Sanctuaries**, including Homhil, Neet, Shu'ab, Detwah, Skand, Sarahin and several areas on the outer islands, while *marine* Nature

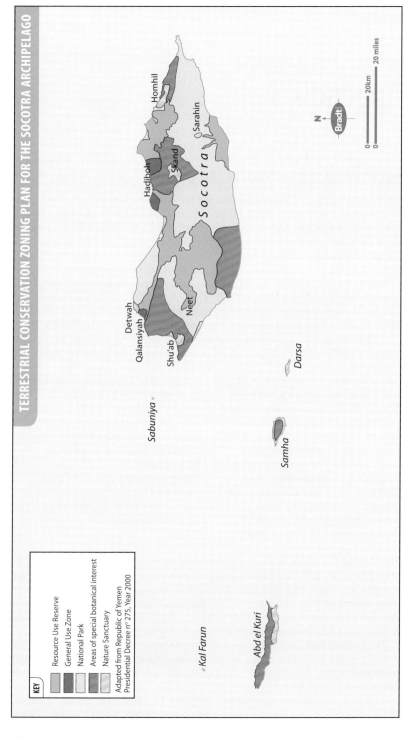

TERRESTRIAL CONSERVATION ZONING PLAN FOR THE SOCOTRA ARCHIPELAGO

KEY

Resource Use Reserve
General Use Zone
National Park
Areas of special botanical interest
Nature Sanctuary

Adapted from Republic of Yemen
Presidential Decree n° 275, Year 2000

Kal Farun

Abd el Kuri

Samha

Darsa

Sabuniya

Qalansiyah
Detwah
Shu'ab
Neet

Hadiboh
Skand
Homhil
Sarahin

S o c o t r a

N
Bradt

0   20km
0   20 miles

Sanctuaries include Rosh and Dihamri. These have the highest level of protection because they contain highly vulnerable species, and even ecotourism infrastructure is restricted here. Most scientists now agree, for example based on studies of reptiles, that far more areas in Socotra should have the highest protection level in order to avoid extinctions. The level between National Park and General Use Zone, called the **Resource Use Reserve**, covers most of the lowlands of the main island.

The Zoning Plan is available to read online. It defines, for each zone, what is allowed and what is not, but also lists more general articles that are important for the entire archipelago. These are not simply guidelines – the Zoning Plan is an actual **law**, and every **visitor** arriving on Socotra is expected, as when visiting other countries, to know the most important, publicly available laws. According to the Zoning Plan, for example, the import of qat is forbidden, as is importing seeds and seedlings without proper analysis and examination by the government (invasive alien species are a real threat to biodiversities on islands!). Some articles relate to **ecotourism**: its capacity and infrastructure should not threaten Socotra's important biodiversity. This means for tourists that arrivals on the island should not exceed its capacity, and it is illegal to cause damage to nature in Socotra. A few important points as defined in the Zoning Plan are given below. The purpose of this law is to:

1. **Protect the biodiversity** of the Socotra archipelago;
2. Achieve a **balance** between the population's development needs and the available natural resources, to avoid negative impact;
3. Preserve the **traditional practices** in management of natural resources;
4. Protect the **nature sanctuaries** in Socotra's islands;
5. Protect the **genetic material** of rare and endemic species on Socotra's islands;
6. Exercise a **sound environmental management** in these areas to protect natural resources from negative impact by development activities.

Besides the Socotra Conservation Zoning Plan, Socotra is of course also protected by a range of important national and international environmental laws, including **CITES**. Therefore, **no live plants or animals, shells, corals and such materials can be taken from the islands** unless under a very specific agreement under pure scientific research. Intensive checks are carried out at the airport when you are leaving, and if you have anything illegal in your luggage – for example that seashell from the beach that you just couldn't resist or that flower you're going to try to plant at home – it will be confiscated; and in this case please be understanding, as the local authorities are just doing their job and acting entirely according to the law. Remember that **Socotra is not a souvenir**, only your beautiful photos and memories of nature are.

FURTHER INFORMATION If you are uncertain about what is or is not legal, ask your guide, check the maps in the Zoning Plan, and feel free to contact and meet staff of the local Environmental Protection Agency, who are in charge of ensuring the Zoning Plan is implemented. The English summary text of the **Socotra Conservation Zoning Plan** plus maps showing the protected areas are available on w socotraproject.org/userfiles/files/Zoning%20plan%20information.pdf.

For more about threats to individual species in Socotra, check the **IUCN Red List** website (w iucnredlist.org) and look for Socotri species. Under the threats per species there are details about general impacts and the importance of conservation.

Documents and info on the Socotra archipelago **UNESCO World Heritage Property** and State of Conservation Reports (highlighting the challenges to the biodiversity) are available here: w whc.unesco.org/en/list/1263.

Appendix 4

CHECKLIST OF ENDEMIC SPECIES IN THIS BOOK
FLORA
Socotran dragon's blood tree (*Dracaena cinnabari*) (page 6) .... ☐
Cucumber tree (*Dendrosicyos socotranus*) (page 6) .... ☐
Desert rose (*Adenium obesum* subsp *sokotranum*) (page 7) .... ☐
Socotran fig (*Dorstenia gigas*) (page 7) .... ☐
Frankincense trees (*Boswellia* spp) (pages 12 & 14) .... ☐
Socotran croton (*Croton socotranus*) (page 5) .... ☐
Jatropha unicostata (Euphorbiaceae family) (page 5) .... ☐
Euphorbia arbuscula (page 12) .... ☐
Duvaliandra dioscorides (succulent asclepiad) (page 7) .... ☐
Socotran begonia (*Begonia socotrana*) (page 7) .... ☐
Persian or Socotran violet (*Exacum affine*) (pages 12 & 94) .... ☐
Socotran pomegranate (*Punica protopunica*) (page 12) .... ☐
Oldenlandia pulvinata (Rubiaceae family) (pages 9 & 94) .... ☐
Lachnocapsa spathulata (Brassicaceae family) (page 113) .... ☐
Hypericum scopulorum (page 9) .... ☐
Hibiscus dioscoridis (page 9) .... ☐
Trichodesma laxiflorum (page 9) .... ☐

FAUNA
Invertebrates
Long-horned grasshopper (*Pyrgomorpha conica*) (page 14) .... ☐
Wingless grasshopper (*Dioscoridus depressus*) (page 14) .... ☐
Giant land snail (*Riebeckiea socotorana*) (page 14) .... ☐
'Tree snail' (*Achatinelloides socotrensis*) (page 14) .... ☐
Caper white butterfly (*Belenois anomala*) (page 14) .... ☐
Swift butterfly (*Charaxes balfouri*) (page 15) .... ☐
Scarlet darter (dragonfly) (*Crocothemis erythraea*) (page 16) .... ☐
Socotran (Grant's) bluet (damselfly) (*Azuragrian granti*) (page 16) .... ☐
Blue baboon spider (*Monocentropus balfouri*) (page 16) .... ☐
Socotra freshwater crab (*Socotrapotamon socotrensis*) (page 19) ...... ☐

Reptiles
Socotra rock gecko (*Pristurus sokotranus*) (page 18) .... ☐
Socotra skink (*Trachylepis socotrana*) (page 19) .... ☐
Socotran chameleon (*Chamaeleo monachus*) (page 19) .... ☐
Dragon's blood tree gecko (*Hemidactylus dracaenacolus*) (page 19) .... ☐

The male Somali starling, in flight here, is almost identical to the endemic Socotran starling, save for the longer, more wedge-shaped tail (page 21) (Chris Miller)

Giant Socotra gecko (*Haemodracon riebeckii*) (page 21) .... ☐
Günther's racer snake (*Ditypophis vivax*) (page 21) .... ☐
Socotran racer snake (*Hemerophis socotrae*) (page 21) .... ☐

Birds *(all on page 27; photos pages 22–3)*
Socotra buzzard (*Buteo socotraensis*) .... ☐
Socotra scops owl (*Otus socotranus*) .... ☐
Socotra starling (*Onychogathus frater*) .... ☐
Socotra bunting (*Emberiza socotrana*) .... ☐
Socotra sunbird (*Chalcomitra balfouri*) .... ☐
Socotra warbler (*Incana incana*) .... ☐
Socotra cisticola (*Cisticola haesitatus*) .... ☐
Socotra sparrow (*Passer insularis*) .... ☐
Abd el Kuri sparrow (*Passer hemileucus*) .... ☐
Socotra golden-winged grosbeak (*Rhynchostruthus socotranus*) .... ☐
Socotra white-eye (*Zosterops socotranus*) .... ☐
Jouanin's petrel (*Bulweria fallax*) .... ☐

For a complete checklist of the all the birds of Socotra, with some photos, visit
w osme.org/2020/04/checklist-of-the-birds-of-the-socotra-archipelago.

Appendix 4 CHECKLIST OF ENDEMIC SPECIES IN THIS BOOK

A4

Index

Entries in **bold** are main entries; those in *italic* refer to maps and those <u>underlined</u> indicate a photo.

INDEX OF ADVERTISERS